Grace Canceled

GRACE CANCELED

How Outrage Is Destroying Lives, Ending Debate, and Endangering Democracy

DANA LOESCH

REGNERY
PUBLISHING
A Division of Salem Media Group

Regnery® is a registered trademark of Salem Communications Holding Corporation

ISBN 978-1-68451-014-6
ebook ISBN 978-1-68451-044-3
LCCN: 2019955222

Published in the United States by
Regnery Publishing
A Division of Salem Media Group
300 New Jersey Ave NW
Washington, DC 20001
www.Regnery.com

Manufactured in the United States of America

10 9 8 7 6 5 4 3 2 1

Books are available in quantity for promotional or premium use. For information on discounts and terms, please visit our website: www.Regnery.com.

To my husband Chris,

for his unwavering loyalty, wise counsel, and love

Contents

Introduction

It's spring 2019, and I'm not in the mood to write this book.

I was in a pretty good place emotionally when I pitched this book. It's easy to discuss grace when the circumstances facilitate it, when your heart is happy, when you've nothing to lose, when the journey is favorable. I'd read a quote from Norm MacDonald on forgiveness and redemption in current society, and it inspired me to draft a book proposal. My publisher was intrigued—it was a different sort of topic, particularly for me, a person well-known for merciless political partisanship and a razor-sharp tongue.

And then life hit my perfectly planned world: My oldest son left for college. A power struggle consumed an issue about which I'm passionate, leaving me a helpless spectator, a casualty in a political storm. I was betrayed by people I thought I could trust.

So right now, I feel no grace toward my fellow man, no interest in his redemptive qualities. In fact, I can't help thinking that returning to my old fire-and-brimstone self, devoid of grace and nuance, would take less effort than clawing out a space for grace every day. Politics and culture have become a war zone, and I'm tired of the daily outrages.

The far left is flirting with a level of violence not seen since the 1960s (or, dare I say, the days of Lincoln?), emboldened by the mainstream left's sanctioning-by-ignoring. The *far* right is hell-bent on confirming the left's opinion of it by mimicking the left's own worst tactics. Another faction of the right is busy patting itself on the back for reciting Democrat talking points on cable news while chyron-labeled as Republicans. Others on the right are just trying to hold the frontline against cancel culture, outrage mobs, and de-platforming while praying for either the sweet meteor of death or Jesus to come quickly.

Right now, as I try to write this book, I have never cared less for keeping or making friends. I have never cared less about political capital. And I have never, *ever* cared less for grace, mercy, forgiveness, or redemption. The temptation to let my burning bridges light the path before me is more alluring than the worst vices. I am working on a book about grace in an industry devoid of it. My firstborn is leaving home happy and confident for college, full of hope and optimism, and as I struggle to acclimate, I'm watching two swampland factions descend into a morass of lawsuits and chaos. I am collateral damage after risking it all—when I didn't need to—because I am so passionate about the issue.

Absolute power corrupts absolutely, and no side or issue is exempt.

"I feel like I just found out that Santa Claus isn't real and that he's also a jack wagon," I remarked once to my husband after a conference call with my attorney.

There is a trail of gasoline within a stone's throw before my feet.

I am holding a match, and the flames are licking my fingers.

● ● ●

A week ago I spoke over the phone with a well-known friend who appears daily on television. We commiserated over the miserable state of discourse, how isolating it all is, and what we would do instead if we just walked away.

"If not us, then who? If not now, then when?" came a plea from within me. I feel we are in these positions for a purpose, a purpose that requires a grace that I have to pray for God to provide daily. Anyone familiar with me knows that grace is not one of my natural traits. In my twenties and part of my thirties, I rejoiced in its absence, and just as I was born into conservatism with the birth of my first child, so was I born into the truer understanding of grace as my oldest child grew.

Grace is hard. I think it's harder to forgive wrongs than to apologize for them. It is so much easier and satisfying to cut someone down, to rhetorically destroy him. God knows I've done my share of that. It's easy to obliterate someone in a debate but much harder to persuade him to share your perspective. You have to bore through ego to do that, and let's face it, many people are too thick-headed. No one wants to admit wrongdoing because apologies are viewed as worthless formalities signifying surrender, and forgiveness is in short supply. People don't want to apologize because other people aren't interested in seeing the wrongdoer redeemed, so what's the point in trying? It's a vicious circle that has produced a rabid binary tribalism in our political discourse and in society at large.

As I said, I'm not feeling very grace-oriented right now in life. I pitched this book in 2017, well before the chaos, and got to work shortly after it was accepted. You're now reading this book several months into the future of my present time. I regretted ever pitching this book to my publisher, Regnery, with whom I have long wanted to work. I go back and forth between torching the premise of it and replacing it with a list like Arya's from *Game of Thrones*. I'm emotionally drained, cantankerous, feeling rather merciless, and would prefer to tell people to do something unflattering to themselves anyplace but near me.

I'd say the timing of this book is a cruel twist of fate, but it's not. It's perfect timing.

It's all the more reason I need to write this book. My willingness to live out my belief in grace is being tested right now. God is not without a sense of humor. That I, of all people, am writing a book on grace is a reason for you to read it. I know what it's like to receive undeserved grace, and so do you. And we all know what it's like to deny it to others. Our society at large is addicted to that feeling right now.

Nuanced, insightful debate is dead, sound bites and outrage rule the news cycle, people are so poisonously partisan that finding common ground is viewed as capitulation and compromise is assumed to include a forfeiture of principle.

Politics used to be a nuisance, but extreme polarization has made it wretched.

My social media timelines and comments are filled by (often verified) partisans who think that typing their invectives in all caps amounts to informed debate. A simple disagreement is an attack on their character. Refusing to affirm their opinion as fact is an affront to decency, a reason for them to boycott, burn, attack, and smear you.

Other Republicans are eager to prove their bona fides to whichever non-Fox cable outlet will identify them as a "contributor." These self-appointed bouncers of the right indict fellow Republicans and conservatives as sellouts for supporting Trump, even as they put aside long-held conservative principles like the right to life, lower taxes, and border security. They preen for the cameras, take screen grabs of their hits for Instagram, and celebrate that people are finally taking them seriously now that they have swapped their poorly-written, vanilla-wafer takes on Republican policy for over-rehearsed, snarky denunciations of the administration and everyone who supports any part of it.

You want a cable contributor deal, a book deal, and your name in the chyron? Talk about how, sure, Trump cut taxes, fueling rapid economic growth, lowered unemployment for every demographic, including high school drop-outs, and actually made good on all the talk about moving the U.S. embassy to Jerusalem, and OK, he expanded the GOP by throwing the tent over blue-collar workers worried about losing their jobs over PC pronouns—*but his tweets!* He cheated on his wife!

And don't forget the "Christian" version, which excoriates believers who like the president's tax cuts, stabilized foreign policy, and record-low unemployment even though he's an admitted fornicator who writes mean things on Twitter.com. We should forfeit the election because of his tweets! Ah, the moral suffering of those poor innocent souls!

"How can Trump be so vulgar?" a vulgar society asks disingenuously. Blaming it all on Trump excuses our culpability for our political culture.

At the Virginia Ratifying Convention, James Madison said, "But I go on this great republican principle, that the people will have virtue and intelligence to select men of virtue and wisdom. Is there no virtue among us? If there be not, we are in a wretched situation. No theoretical checks—no form of government can render us secure. To suppose that any form of government will secure liberty or happiness without any virtue in the people, is a chimerical idea. If there be sufficient virtue and intelligence in the community, it will be exercised in the selection of these men. So that we do not depend on their virtue, or put confidence in our rulers, but in the people who are to choose them."

George Washington echoed the sentiment: "Human rights can only be assured among a virtuous people. The general government ... can never be in danger of degenerating into a monarchy, an oligarchy, an aristocracy, or any despotic or oppressive form so long as there is any virtue in the body of the people."

Montesquieu wrote, "When virtue is banished, ambition invades the minds of those who are disposed to receive it, and avarice possesses the whole community."

The virtuous man isn't a man without fault but a man who admits his fault. What good are apologies in a post-redemption world?

Why do people expect a leader to meet a standard of virtue they themselves are unwilling to meet? What sort of leaders does such a society produce?

We're in an era of red meat platitudes, when one can parrot phrases from popular conservative websites, intellectual discussion is brushed aside for hyper-edited, gimmicky shtick, no one has the attention span to watch a YouTube video longer than two minutes, former friends and allies turn into caricatures of their former selves because power, or proximity to it, is a helluva drug.

It is in this environment that I'm desperately searching for grace within.

Grace isn't given easily, not at first. In the beginning, I resented how I was treated by people who deserved to have coals of fire heaped on their heads. But then my oldest son became a teenager. His world expanded beyond cartoons and juice boxes. He was *in* the world now, subject to however the adults before him had shaped it—not only him, but his sweet friends, too. They are stepping into our cancel culture society, our de-platforming society, a society where no one talks because everyone is hoarse from screaming, where you're all in or all out, a society of adults eager to tear them apart over any transgression from their adolescence—not out of real concern for the transgression, but because it's fun to tear people apart. This is the lesson for our youth: They will never be redeemed, never be greater than their lowest moment, never forgiven for anything, ever. It's not enough to win someone over. He must be destroyed professionally, financially, emotionally, everyone he knows turned against him for the sin of ever holding a different opinion.

We don't allow grace or forgiveness now for each other, so how are we to ever teach the next generation that it ever existed?

CHAPTER ONE

American Tribalism

And I went down to the demonstration
To get my fair share of abuse,
Singing, "We're gonna vent our frustration
If we don't we're gonna blow a fifty-amp fuse."

—*The Rolling Stones, "You Can't Always Get What You Want"*

No one ever imagined that a ginger braggart with a thick New York accent, a romancer of women who looked like Robert Palmer's video vixens, a guy who was once friendly with Al Sharpton and played the game with both Democrats and Republicans, was presidential material —much less that he would actually become president. Everyone assumed that the office of president was closely guarded. Beyond the bare constitutional requirements, you had to check certain boxes, namely:

- look like you stepped out of a Vineyard Vines ad
- Ivy League diploma
- picture-perfect nuclear family that telegraphs trustworthiness, dependability, and commercial appeal
- transgressions hidden away

There was one more rule: never defend yourself; leave that to surrogates. These rules were so firmly established that few took Trump seriously when he announced his candidacy in 2015. To the Republican Party, he was vulgar. And ever since the waning days of the 2016 general election campaign, countless Republican office-holders, operatives, high-dollar donors, pundits, and other political Statlers and Waldorfs have been wringing their hands over Trump.

"He's ruining our brand!" they lament to each other through their columns.

"I would rather any Democratic 2020 candidate than him," scoffed these bouncers of the party. If Trump was pro-life these Republicans couldn't identify as pro-life. If Trump was for free markets, these Republicans couldn't support free markets. If Trump derided gun control, these Republicans were suddenly pro–gun control. When Trump cited Scripture as "Two Corinthians" instead of "Second Corinthians," the Republican Pharisees gracelessly scoffed and patted themselves on the back for loving Jesus more than Trump does. These Republicans are more wedded to the image of a Republican president than to the principles that president might advance. So weak are their conservative moorings that their previously held positions on abortion and the Second Amendment fell away in the face of a Trump tweet. Is Trump that powerful, or are they just that weak?

"Our precious, valuable brand!" they cry. But what was the GOP brand? More conservative voters felt that the party tainted their brand decades ago by supporting out-of-control spending, big government policies like No Child Left Behind, and compromises on important economic issues.

If Trump is vulgar in tweets, the GOP has been vulgar in policy.

In the 2016 Republican presidential primaries, I supported Rick Perry, the former governor of Texas, in part because I felt governors were better prepared for presidential duties due to the similarities between their role and the role of the executive. After Perry dropped out I supported Senator Ted Cruz because I felt he would aggressively protect individual liberties and our (quasi-) capitalist system. I supported Trump in the general election and hoped he would allay my concerns about his murky record on certain crucial issues. I like the idea of someone from outside the Beltway in the Oval Office, but with that comes a measure of mystery. Where will he come down on issues such as life, the Second Amendment, and faith? I wanted to be proved wrong. I wanted voters to feel vindicated by their choice at the ballot box. I wanted Trump's successful first term to unify a fractured American right.

It was frustrating to see a smaller group of Republicans—some of them driven by genuine convictions about Trump's approach that I may not share, the others stubbornly refusing to recognize that sometimes their assumptions were wrong—position themselves as conservatism's bouncers, attacking Trump voters on cable news at least as often as they attacked the Democrats. Many of these malcontents had raised their eyebrows at Tea Partiers—the unwashed masses who were too provincial to understand policy much less demand a seat at the national table. They treated us as party crashers. When Tea Partiers endorsed candidates, the bouncers declared them unqualified and ran their own establishment candidates, often with disastrous results (see New York's Twenty-third Congressional District with Dede Scozzafava). When Tea Partiers won the House for the GOP in 2010, these self-styled Republican babysitters were forced to admit that grassroots tactics not only had succeeded but had given new life to an aging party that had appeared to be riding off into the sunset.

In time, the two sides became allies, more or less, until 2016. Trump was richer than most of the stereotypical Republican elite, but he did reality television and was not a blue blood. He was also known as a notorious philanderer (notorious because he himself discussed it). Many of the GOP snobs would overlook the indiscretions of the right kind of politician, but not if it was Trump.

One of those politicians is Mark Sanford, the former governor of South Carolina, who in August 2019 told CNN's Jake Tapper that people who "have said we need to have a conversation about what it means to be a Republican" had encouraged him to challenge Trump in the 2020 primaries.[1] He added, "The bent that we've been moving toward here of late is not consistent with the values and the ideals they believed in for a very long time." He announced his candidacy the following month, explaining that voters are "weary of the bully in the schoolyard routine," before dropping out in November of 2019.

Just as, I'm sure, they're weary of the "Appalachian Trail" excuse. When voters think "Sanford" they don't think "principle." They think of the week in 2009 when the governor disappeared, supposedly because he was "hiking the Appalachian Trail." The trail, it turned out, led to his mistress's bedroom in Argentina, to which he had traveled on the taxpayers' dime.

A caller to my radio show explained why voters like her could still support Trump after his highly publicized affair in the 1990s: "He never ran from it." She added that unlike "the first Bush, Clinton, some of these others, he didn't hide what he did. He owned it outright and never pretended that he was something he wasn't." Trump didn't check his thoughts; he lacked the preferred social graces; he threw punches; he was unorthodox, argumentative, vindictive, and temperamental; and he demanded unquestionable loyalty, which most Republicans today are too weak to demand and too weak to give in return.

My caller's praise of Trump's fighting spirit was especially telling. Middle Americans were finished with being ridiculed, smeared, and denigrated for asking questions about their health care, taxes, Iran, and gun-running across the southern border. Every time Middle Americans disagreed with President Obama, they were called "racists." Even though half the country voted enthusiastically for our first black president, somehow we were so racist he couldn't implement his agenda, and when he was successful implementing his agenda—the billion-dollar-boondoggle of a healthcare website, for instance—and failures resulted, the failures were pinned on Bush—Obama had *inherited* the problems. Keep in mind that a good portion of these Middle Americans are union folks. They backed Clinton in the 1990s and early 2000s. They left only when Bill's overbearing and unlikable wife determined it was her turn to run for public office.

Blue-collar voters, who had turned out twice for Bill Clinton and then for Al Gore, felt an aversion to Hillary. I'll never forget the

security-camera video of her and her longtime aide Huma Abedin standing in line at a Chipotle restaurant in Maumee, Ohio, where Hillary was
seen staring down the employees making her food from behind her huge,
bug-eyed movie-star sunglasses. The restaurant employees never realized
she was there until a reporter informed them hours later.[2] At least she
visited Ohio. She skipped Wisconsin, which surprised the country on
election day by going for Trump.

Clinton later blamed her loss in Wisconsin on racism (which even
the left-leaning Politifact debunked),[3] but she lost because she didn't
connect with its people. Lecturing voters on sexism, pronouns, and
bathrooms while Obamacare sends their insurance premiums through
the roof and cuts them off from their doctors, while their hometown jobs
disappear, and while manufacturing moves overseas is not a winning
strategy. Hillary focused on rich people's problems. Transgender-friendly
bathroom policies don't pay premiums, grocery bills, utility bills, or
automobile bills, and they don't finance anyone's retirement.

Voters saw that Obama's infamous "bitter clinger" comment was
more than just a passing remark. It revealed how the Democratic Party
views the people it keeps at arm's length but needs for electoral wins.
Democrats' biggest downfall is their inability to recognize their short-
comings when conducting these electoral postmortems.

Democrats lost so many blue-collar workers in 2016 for a reason
that they fail to understand at their own peril. Instead of acknowledging
the problem of lost manufacturing jobs and soaring health care premiums, they focused on feminism, race, and inequality. Many white blue-
collar workers already felt pretty unequal as they watched their ability
to live paycheck to paycheck diminish. Many Hispanic Americans felt
unequal as politicians ignored them to accommodate those entering
illegally. And many black Americans felt unequal as their unemployment
rate rose under the nation's first black president and black children were
gunned down in gang and drug violence. As I noted in my book *Flyover
Nation*, these voters were good enough to vote twice for Bill Clinton,
good enough to support Al Gore, and good enough to turn out for

Barack Obama, but because they couldn't pull the lever for Hillary Clinton they were all declared sexists and racists in 2016.

Rolling into 2020 the strategy was the same. Bill Clinton's onetime press secretary Joe Lockhart tweeted with characteristic subtlety, "Anyone who supports a racist or a racist strategy is a racist themselves [sic]. 2020 is a moment of reckoning for America. Vote for Donald Trump, and you are a racist. Don't hide it like a coward. Wear that racist badge proudly and see how it feels."[4]

MSNBC's Chris Hayes added, "But the base, what does the base get? The folks in that arena. Well, it's obvious, isn't it? They get to chant. They get to revel in their own Americanness and primacy at the expense of others." Not only is the base at fault for their patriotism and desire to protect their country, but "Trump and now the entire Republican Party and most of the conservative movement realize that is enough for them."[5] He added that the voting base should be destroyed: "It must be peacefully, nonviolently, politically destroyed with love, compassion, and determination, but utterly confronted and destroyed. That is the only way to break the coalition apart."

Congresswoman Marcia Fudge, a Democrat from Ohio, declared on the House floor that Trump voters are "racist, steeped in religious beliefs, ignorant, or … just plain dumb."[6]

On CNN, the progressive journalist Kirsten Powers bemoaned Trump's female supporters: "I think that we would hope that we would get better behavior from white women because white women are themselves oppressed and that they would be able to align themselves with other oppressed people. I think we have to remember that the white patriarchal system actually benefits white women in a lot of ways, and they are attached to white men who are benefiting from the system that was created by them, for them. And their fathers and their husbands and their brothers are benefiting from the system, and so they are also benefiting."[7] The Democratic presidential contenders piled on. The Irish-American Robert "Beto" O'Rourke declared that the act of voting for Trump was racist.[8]

The media gleefully participate in the campaign of emotional terror-ism. "ANGER AT BEING LABELED RACIST IS THE NEW 'CUL-TURAL ANXIETY' FOR TRUMP SUPPORTERS," blared a *Washington Post* headline.[9] Is it any wonder that voters—especially in flyover nation—are rejecting the news media and the Democratic Party after years of loyal support?

Stunned Democrats picked up on the "bad orange man is a racist" theme on election night of 2016. Racism—with plenty of sexism thrown in for good measure—had to be responsible for Hillary's loss. The people (about half of them white), who had supported her husband through his sex scandals and elected the first black president, were racist, sexist "deplorables." Hillary attributed her failure to the people whose own voting record made her run possible in the first place. Blue-collar voters felt betrayed—and confused. They didn't vote for the blonde white woman, so they were ... racists? They judged her on merit and not on sex, so they were ... sexist? There were 62,984,825 people who voted for Trump in 2016. And every one of them was a racist and a sexist?

It was Hillary who demanded exemption from responsibility for her actions because of her sex, yet it was the voters who were sexist. Much of the left followed her lead, despite having fêted Trump over the years. The celebrity tycoon, star of *The Apprentice*, had been a fixture of popu-lar culture. He was name-checked in songs. He made "You're fired!" a catch phrase. But his announcement that he was running for president as a Republican ended this acceptance. No grace, no tolerance is extended to anyone who takes a position contrary to that of Hollywood and the Democratic Party. It's the one unforgivable sin.

In other words, close but no cigar.

While Democrats have always relied on some form of identity poli-tics, today it constitutes the entirety of their platform.

I was in grade school when Reagan was president, and I remember one of my little friends and her twin sister telling me at recess that Reagan had stolen their grandparents' jobs and money was tight. That's what their mother had told them when they asked why they couldn't attend

an event at the town roller rink. It was my first political conversation. I
didn't know much about Reagan at the time, but from their remarks he
sounded like a giant in the sky, sticking his big Republican hand down
to earth to scoop up all these people's jobs.

When my mom picked me up from school in her third-hand car that
needed prayer as much as fuel to get up steep hills, I asked her if Reagan
was the reason I couldn't go to the event at the roller rink. Her answer
had something to do with child support, not Reagan, and that's about
all I remember of it, but that's my first memory of politics. Reagan hated
poor people. He was a Republican. So Republicans hated poor people.
I was raised in a Democrat family, and most of my teachers were Democrats, including my favorite one. Most of my friends and their families
were Democrats. It was easy to remain insulated. That stereotype of
Republicans was like a tree that added a ring every year, growing stronger and thicker. My perception of the party grew narrower with the
accretion of each new prejudice. By the time I was in college, I was,
against all sense and reason, a liberal. Not the good Tocqueville kind,
but more like a progressive, save for gun rights, the only consistent position in my life.

My political brainwashing lasted until I reached my twenties, when
two things rocked my world. Childbirth cemented my views on abortion,
and 9/11 cemented my views on every other political issue. The only
Republican I knew growing up was a brilliant boy whose life was tragically cut short in a car accident. He was the first contradiction to my
long-held stereotype of Republicans, which I realized only after he was
gone. Smart, kind, from a middle-class family, he argued George H. W.
Bush logic to my Bill Clinton emotion in the journalism class we both
took. Unlike me, he never got angry during our debates. I wasn't exposed
to other Republican or conservative ideas until college. Slowly, brick by
brick, my stereotype of those who thought differently than I did on political issues was deconstructed. The more educated I became, the more
open-minded I grew. I left the Democratic Party so gradually, I hardly
realized how far I had gone until 9/11.

The most difficult thing for me after leaving was reclaiming any common ground with the left. The left I had known had faded away, replaced by a caricature of a socialist party, its worst attributes intensified by the Internet.

I am not sure how the leftists I knew then stayed with the party, but many are still there. What happened in their hearts and minds to move so far left on individual rights? To reject pro-life members of their party? What are they really protecting by locking arms and standing as one if they've had to abandon their most deeply cherished beliefs to move further left? What have they lost by refusing to embrace any common ground with those on the right, by refusing to see people as still people, even if they disagree with them on economic policy?

When Joe Scarborough, who hates my guts (and whom I'm honestly not very fond of either), met Paul McCartney, someone yelled to the singer that Scarborough was a Republican, which is ideological leprosy in the entertainment industry.[10] Scarborough was escorted out of the room. Whenever the left enters the public space, it attributes all evil in the world to whomever it disagrees with, so where do you go from there? How does a conversation take place when one side refuses to acknowledge the humanity of the other side?

The biggest and best thing the left ever did was to brand its ideology. Conservatives just let them do it. Democrats branded themselves in the arts and entertainment, culture, and trends. They came up with cool logos and slogans, but their actual product—their policy proposals and their ideology—was the proverbial turd in the punchbowl. But that doesn't matter to people who vote on feeling rather than fact. These are the same people who will purchase wine because the label looks cool. Think about it: brands like Apple and Harley-Davidson are more than just products; they're statements about your life.

People love to advertise themselves to other people. They love making public pronouncements about their beliefs—what they like, their aesthetic, their politics—to anyone who will listen. Democrats have taken advantage of that with appealing branding. For crying out loud, Obama's slogan was "hope and change"! No one ever stopped to ask, "What change?" Change from what? Good change? Bad change? Neutral, lateral change? Doesn't matter! It follows hope! Hope suggests it's good change! Whoo! I can't honestly remember what the GOP slogan was in 2008 or 2012. The GOP doesn't grasp the power of branding. Branding is nothing more than formalizing a consistent identity. Democrats have been so successful at it they decided to essentially trademark entire ethnicities as their brand, too, producing a new and highly effective strategy called identity politics.

Identity politics has paralyzed American conversation, and we're all dumber for it. People are terrified of offending others. It should infuriate us that so many people are afraid to speak out for fear of being unfairly targeted. Think about it: Who are the people who are afraid of offending others? Good and decent people. No decent person wants to treat anyone else badly. It pains him to give offense. Most people are decent—but if I'm being honest, that view is challenged every time the militant left appeals to the morality of good people to con them into believing they are committing phantom offenses. It is reprehensible to accuse people of racism for voting for a candidate you dislike, and it trivializes a real evil. Rasmussen released a poll in July 2019 showing that 32 percent of Democrats believe that any disagreement with a politician of color is racist.[11] That same week Politico argued for an increase in the minimum wage because tipping is racist.[12] What is racism if everything is racist? Progressives, particularly white progressives, have made the term a blunt weapon. Now "racist" is used to describe everything from disagreeing on health care to criticizing a politician's policy proposal if that politician is a minority.

Los Angeles media reported that the neighbors of the two San Bernardino terrorists, Syed Rizwan Farook and Tashfeen Malik, didn't tell authorities about the pair's suspicious behavior because they were afraid—not of terrorists, but of being viewed as racists.[13] The same political correctness let Major Nidal Hasan roam loose at Fort Hood, where he eventually murdered thirteen people, despite numerous indications that he was a threat.[14]

Tribalism and its chief tool, identity politics, have made our citizens incapable of even identifying threats for fear of being considered racist—even though all people, not just white people, are hurt by such evil. Since everything, even the most benign and most inoffensive remarks, might provoke outrage, offending people is now Americans' worst fear.

Political identification is a fun study of marketing and psychology. As I said earlier, it's branding. Because most people are too lazy to think, they make a decision about a person's character the moment they learn his political affiliation. For decades, Democrats have worked hard to brand not only themselves but also Republicans. You cannot be considered authentically female, black, Hispanic, gay, trans, etc., unless you are a Democrat. Anyone who falls into one of those categories and is *not* a Democrat is ridiculed in the press and on social media as a sell-out or worse.

To think the worst of someone's remarks or motives, not only must grace be denied, but it must be assumed that grace cannot exist. People must be divided, common ground obscured. The left reinforces these political divisions by pushing not just ideological segregation, but ethnic segregation too. The more they can present you as an issue instead of a person, a demographic instead of an individual, the easier it is for them to institute tribal division. Identity is a weapon, and victimhood is a currency. Identity politics and its byproduct of hyper-political correctness have resulted in the death of comedy, the death of nuance (more on that later), and most importantly, the death of forgiveness, redemption, and common ground.

When it was announced that Sean Spicer was to appear on ABC's *Dancing with the Stars*, the left armed itself with torches and pitchforks and took to social media and the press. It's easier for people to dehumanize others by reducing them to mere issues. Spicer's fellow competitor and the star of *Queer Eye*, Karamo Brown, said he speaks regularly with Spicer and was eager to show the country how two people of such different backgrounds and beliefs can come together and get along. "I'm a big believer that if you can talk to someone and meet in the middle, you can learn about each other and help each other both grow. We have been chatting all day today—he's a good guy, a really sweet guy," Brown told Access Hollywood.

Brown committed the awful sin of stating that someone who thinks differently than he does on policy issues could—gasp—still be a "good guy." The rage mob once again armed themselves with torches and pitchforks and went to work righting this mighty wrong. They were successful to some extent: Brown was forced to delete his Twitter account and suspend comments on his Instagram account because of the hatred from those on the left. Brown addressed his haters on Twitter:

> First, I have no say who is on the cast and didn't find out till this morning that he is on. But I'll tell you this ... I'm excited to sit down [with] him and engage in respectful conversations. Only way things get better is if we try to educate those who have different [points of view] than us. But I understand how my comments could lead people to believe that I don't understand the gravity of the situation. The personal is political. I'm reminded of it daily as a gay man of color. I know that representation matters—that it can affect change. I see you [and] I hear you. I'm bringing my personal message of love, equity, [and] inclusion to the dance floor. I want it to eclipse [and] triumph over divisiveness [and] hatred[15]

Brown followed up with an Instagram post to his haters:

> So ... some of you may know I deleted my other social media pages and took a long break from posting on ig because I been in a bad state of mind. My kids/family & I were being threatened by strangers.... People who I thought supported & loved me turned their backs on me ... saying I was a traitor, a horrible person, delusional and treating me really bad ... but as

I walk into my first dance rehearsal for @dancingabc No More Tears and No More Holding My Head Low!

Spicer remarked on the backlash to the press:

He and I had a really fun talk—not about politics, just about getting to know each other and how excited we are about that opportunity. That's kind of been his trademark. He has tried to foster a more positive dialogue and he did it again and it was really great, but I felt bad because he was trying to be a good person. He was obviously doing the right and good thing and he has the best intentions. We need more people like him as opposed to fewer. It was a shame that people were so nasty to him.[16]

Those who've made an industry out of "tolerance" and "inclusion" didn't want to give Brown the opportunity to give someone else a chance.

When it was announced that David Mamet's *American Buffalo* was returning to Broadway, cranky theater wokescolds protested.[17] The Pulitzer Prize–winning Mamet is the premier screenwriter and playwright in America, the author of such influential plays as *Glengarry Glen Ross* and *Speed-the-Plow* and such films as *The Untouchables*, *Hoffa*, *Hannibal*, and *The Postman Always Rings Twice*. But because Mamet came out of the closet as a conservative—first with an explosive *Village Voice* op-ed titled "Why I am No Longer A 'Brain-Dead' Liberal" and then with the book *The Secret Knowledge: On the Dismantling of American Culture*—some in theater wanted to make him the latest victim of cancel-culture. Mamet's work is so influential and his legacy inextinguishable, so he is protected from the rage mob—not that they won't try. There is no acceptance of anything other than full surrender, full assimilation. Anything else in one's life is nullified by the evil presence of a dissenting opinion. Acknowledging any common ground is betrayal.

Progressives don't believe that it's "tolerance" if what's being tolerated is the viewpoint of a conservative, a Republican, a libertarian, or
an independent. It's not true "diversity" unless everyone thinks the same
as they do. There is no room for grace in this tribalism because grace
requires that you see the person for the individual he is instead of just a
walking, talking issue. Tribalism encourages the view that forgiveness is
betrayal and redemption is out of reach. Forgiveness has been reinter-
preted to mean "compromise," and "compromise" is just a longer word
for "betrayal." To train people against forgiveness and common ground,
which destroy tribal barriers, leftists treat forgiveness as worse than tolerance—it's acceptance, sanction, and ownership of an offense. To forgive
is to make someone's offense your own, making you as bad as the
offender. People are terrified. They see that they have nothing to gain
from forgiveness, so tribalism and gracelessness are reinforced, stronger
than before. The rage mob are the bouncers.

Oddly enough, while Democrat politicians revel in and cater to
identity politics, their voters don't as much. An April 2019 Monmouth
survey concluded, "Race and gender do not seem to be important factors
for Democratic voters when considering who[m] the party should choose
to run against Trump. Fully 87% say the race of the nominee does not
matter."[18]

This perhaps explains the Teflon coating of Ralph Northam and
Elizabeth Warren. White Democrats have the ultimate privilege.
Northam (I refer to him as "Governor Blackface Abortham" on the
radio), the governor of Virginia, was discovered in some compromising
medical school yearbook photographs that featured him and a friend in
blackface and dressed as a Klansman. In a subsequent press conference
Northam admitted it was he in the photos and that he had worn blackface often before, once as Michael Jackson. (He offered to demonstrate
the moonwalk for the assembled reporters before his wife sensibly
stopped what would have been the GIF of the year.) The result was a lot
of shocked and outraged Republicans and conservatives, both black and
white, and an apathetic Democratic Party, which shrugged and sent

Northam on a "Sorry about the blackface" statewide tour—but only when they realized his later comments about "post-birth abortion" (what thinking people call "murder") on a local radio show were more problematic than his student blackface days, so their safest strategy is to play up the blackface.

Elizabeth Warren identified herself as an American Indian in directories used for hiring law professors. Warren Jacobson at Legal Insurrection did yeoman's researching her background, noting:

> Warren stopped filling out the law professor directory as Native American when she gained a full-time tenured job at Harvard Law School in the mid-1990s. At that point, being Native American and a supposed-minority no longer was needed, Warren had reached the top rung of the law professor ladder. While Warren asserts that she never actually gained an advantage from claiming to be Native American and a minority, there is no doubt that she tried to gain an advantage. When that need for advantage was over, she dropped the designation.[19]

Warren used Native Americans when she needed them professionally and then dropped them.

She tried defending herself by passing off a pilfered recipe in a cookbook titled *Pow-Wow Chow* and citing her high cheekbones (since her Swiss Miss blonde hair and blue eyes were insufficient). On NBC, Warren told a whopper of a tale accusing her own grandparents of racism that drove her "minority" mother and white father to elope—a tale disputed by the Cherokee genealogist Twila Barnes.[20] Warren then staged a theatrically ridiculous DNA test, the results of which told her she was whiter than Ikea and the hygge concept, and she finally somewhat copped to making the story up. Democrats did not condemn her or demand that she apologize to the indigenous nations she dodged at events, whose invitations to meet she regularly spurned.

Warren was never held accountable by her party because Democrats are concerned about racial issues only when the perception that they care about race is threatened. If Trump is a racist because he is a Republican, then surely Ralph Northam is a racist for wearing blackface. If Trump is a racist because he ran for president against an older white woman, then surely Elizabeth Warren is a racist for masquerading as a member of a tribal nation for the sake of professional advancement.

SJWs never formed a rage mob to come for Warren or Northam. Intersectionality, identity politics is meaningless when it concerns leftist politicians.

The majority of Democrat voters don't care how many coveted intersectional boxes candidates tick off; they just want someone capable who can do the job—a fact that reveals the power of social media to mask reality. In September 2019, a Gallup survey found an 86-point gap between Democrats and Republicans in the approval of President Trump, the highest measure of polarization on record.[21] The political tribalism cuts deep. As former Secretary of Defense James Mattis has smartly observed,

> When we run elections, it's always about dividing. "I'm smart, you're not." "I'm wise and you're dumb." It's not always pretty, it's not always civil. Well, welcome to democracy. Once an election's over, you go into governance, and it's not about divisiveness, it's about unity … but we no longer seem to go to governance. It's like we're in a constant election mode and constantly finding reason to cheer against each other instead of working together.[22]

We are stuck in a post-election "failure to launch" phase, orchestrated by those who would invalidate elections by substituting division and furor for voter enthusiasm. They have made it impossible for the country to come together on much of anything. Earlier in 2019, as *Game of Thrones* finished its final season, I noted to friends with whom we watched the final season that the series seems like that last cultural touchpoint we could share as a country, the last "must-see" TV that everyone you know watched. Netflix, Hulu, Amazon TV, and other streaming services leave us so segregated that we have nothing left to talk about. Is *Stranger Things* the last show the country is watching together?

One spring Sunday my family and I sat in church listening to a sermon on unity. I was particularly interested in my oldest son's hearing it, as he was to head off to college a couple of months later. When I was in college, students congregated in groups based on beliefs, certain shared experiences, and athletics, but none of these affiliations superseded our identity as students at the same school. We were friends and comrades regardless of our religious or political views. Common ground was plentiful and appreciated. We looked for ways we could be reconciled instead of estranged. In hindsight, the fault lines were there. But it doesn't compare to what my son and countless other young collegians experience today.

A person's identity is now based on his social class and on a buzzword coined in 1989, "intersectionality." To be quick and plain, intersectionality is a Marxist concept that calculates a person's power in society based on the demographic groups—racial, ethnic, sexual, and so on—with which said person can claim affiliation. A legless white lesbian is deemed more powerful than a legless black lesbian because of her "white privilege." Meanwhile, a legless black trans woman is less powerful than the legless black lesbian. The black lesbian, after all, is cisgender, meaning she identifies as a woman because she was born a woman, and everybody knows that's quite a privilege.

At least, that's how we see it nowadays. As we embrace intersectionality, no one can celebrate somebody else's culture without provoking the ire of the rage mob, who scream, "Appropriation!" A few years ago, there was even a national cultural argument over whether white women should wear gold hoop earrings.

The problem with identity politics and intersectionality is this: things that have identified and defined a culture are now used as barriers to prevent fellowship with one another. In Galatians 3:28, Paul writes, "There is neither Jew nor Gentile, neither slave nor free, nor is there male and female, for you are all one in Christ Jesus."

The best nationalism, the best tribalism, is that of the kingdom. If people couldn't identify as children of God, they might at least identify first as Americans. But now the very concept of America and her guiding principles are under assault, their legitimacy questioned as each moment in history is retroactively judged by standards of the modern era. Impugning the character of the founders who asserted our unalienable rights, we call into question those rights themselves, as if the legitimacy of the latter had anything to do with the former. There is an all-out war against every tie that would hold us all together.

The left's increasing partisanship, its hyperbole, its devotion to party above country and to the state above the individual, have hardened its heart and closed its ears to dialogue, driving the right to resentment so deep that some conservatives have begun to appropriate the venom and vindictiveness of the left. That's why so much fire and brimstone are spit on cable news and most of talk radio, why news reports are virtually indistinguishable from editorials. This partisanship has driven intelligent people to sell out their smarts. In short, by sacrificing nuance on the altar of partisanship, we've established a dangerous idiocracy.

CHAPTER TWO

Socialist Wave

*"We can't help everyone, but everyone can
help someone."*

—*Ronald Reagan*

B ill Clinton was the last moderate Democrat to hold elected office and likely the last moderate Democrat the country will ever see at the presidential level. Bill Clinton of the *nineties*, that is. Even Barack Obama hid his true ideological colors until *after* assuming office. His apparently moderate social platform (remember, he opposed same-sex marriage) tempered his socialist economic policies, calming the nerves of Democrats too nervous to fully embrace progressivism, that political purgatory between Democrat-liberalism and socialism.

The Democratic Party has changed quite a bit since Bill Clinton was in the White House and has shifted farther to the left since Obama. Candidates are openly proclaiming their socialism and winning seats by doing so. In 2016, the Democratic Socialists of America won major victories[1] in numerous races across the country and made history by sending members of its party to Congress for the first time as Democrats: Rashida Tlaib and Alexandria Ocasio Cortez, who make up one-half of the "Squad."

Cortez's first move out of the gate was to push the "Green New Deal," an omnibus measure that would ban "farting cows" and guarantee incomes to those "unwilling to work." After—and only after—it was widely ridiculed did Cortez blame a "staffer" (sure, sure) for posting it to her congressional website and sending it to all the media, along with all the Democrat presidential primary candidates, most of whom fell all over themselves trying to endorse it the fastest for the first-place virtue-signaling ribbon.[2]

The Democrats who could do math distanced themselves from the Green New Deal because it was positively insane. It proposed eliminating the internal combustion engine, moving the United States entirely to "green" energy, and bankrupting the country. After weeks of Democratic fear-mongering, the Senate majority leader, Mitch McConnell, brought the measure to a vote. Suddenly, the party whose primary candidates were falling all over themselves to endorse the Green New Deal couldn't bring itself actually to support it on the Senate floor. The Democrats realized that supporting the Green New Deal would put them on record as nuts, reducing the 2020 general election to a formality.

As Democrats move farther and farther to the left, so do their rhetoric and tactics.

Socialists' two favorite rhetorical tools are envy and shame, and the platform they build on is identity politics. Of course, a major problem with identity politics is that by definition it excludes grace. It's culturally sanctioned prejudice. People who come from intact families, better neighborhoods, and a generally stable environment are viewed as deserving punishment. They've already enjoyed their share of grace.

Identity politics is a tactic of statists, who foster resentment and envy and then peddle the lie that a bigger government can make everything *fairer*. These feelings justify the cruelty inherent in identity politics. Democrats' favorite tactic is smearing as a "racist" anyone who disagrees with them, challenges their opinion, or simply exists while thinking different thoughts.

Racist is a dirty, heavy term, a term for those with some of the worst moral deficiencies. No one wants to associate himself with a person who thinks his skin color is a self-made accomplishment rather than the product of chance. The idea of racial supremacy is an *unchristian* view entirely contradicted by the Gospels. While everyone is a child of God, racism promotes the supremacy of one over another, making identity an idol and supplanting God in the order of sovereignty and worship. God did not make one of his children more redeemable than the other. The belief and practice of racism contradict that.

It is a sin.

To falsely accuse someone of such a moral deficiency is also a sin.

It is grossly immoral to claim you oppose racism for the evil it is while falsely accusing someone of it—not because you believe that person to be racist, but because you cannot engage in a clash of ideals and hold your own without trying to injure the other person's character and reputation.

That's why, during the days of the Tea Party movement, we reacted with such righteous anger when the term was maliciously applied to us for simply disagreeing with President Obama on health care. "It's because Obama proposed it, and he's the first black president, that's why," the left responded. We opposed government control of healthcare when white Mitt Romney implemented it as governor of Massachusetts, too. But that didn't matter. The left repeated the smear enough to make it stick in the minds of some.

Someone once said to me on cable news that I opposed Obamacare because Obama was black—an absurd argument that equated policy with ethnicity. Democrats for years have tried to inoculate themselves from legitimate criticism of their policies or behavior by invoking race and sex. That reasoning itself is racist because it presupposes that the race of a policy's proponent has some relevance to the policy being pro-posed. Would the former president's healthcare law be *less* likely to pave the way for single-payer if a white Democrat president had proposed it? Was it less so because a white Republican promoted it in Massachusetts? It's a silly question that deserves a silly answer, but silliness has replaced the AP Stylebook. The policy isn't the race of the person who proposed—but Democrats realized that if they could convince voters that it was, they'd have an easier time defending it. Make voters see only race, only identity, not the issue, and the discussion and support will be easier to control.

In July 2019 President Trump responded to a political attack by Congressman Elijah Cummings with a series of tweets about the failed leadership of Baltimore, the city Cummings represented. His "district is a disgusting rat and rodents infested mess," the president tweeted. "If he spent more time in Baltimore, maybe he could help clean up this very dangerous and filthy place." Cummings clapped back, predictably calling Trump a racist. As the headlines tried to out-shriek each other, some of us asked the key question: How is what Trump tweeted in any way "racist?"

Baltimore, a beautiful town I visited in my twenties (having the requisite gothic picture of myself taken at Edgar Allan Poe's grave), has serious problems—problems that Democrats have publicly acknowledged for years. But recognizing those problems becomes racist only when Trump does it. The city's former mayor Catherine Pugh, touring run-down parts of the city, exclaimed to the television cameras, "What the hell? We should just take all this [expletive] down.... Whoa, you can smell the rats.... Whew Jesus.... Oh my G-d, you can smell the dead animals."[3] The city's own daily newspaper reported, "There were 342 homicides in Baltimore last year [2017], 56 per 100,000 people who live in the city. That's the highest per capita in the city's history and, according to the FBI report Monday, the highest rate of any American city with more than 500,000 people. It's also significantly higher than the rate in other big cities."[4]

As in nearly all of our big cities, only one political party has been in charge in Baltimore, and it's not the Republicans, who amount to 8 percent of the vote.[5] Baltimore lost eight thousand residents between 2017 and 2018 as people who could fled for safer, cleaner streets and more responsive representatives.[6]

Trump wasn't wrong about Baltimore, and he wasn't speaking of race. The socialist ideology is ruining Baltimore, my hometown of St.

Louis, Chicago, and many other cities. The media smartly ran interference for Democrats, pretending that his criticism was about race, not the disastrous policies of Congressman Cummings and the rest of his party. With every major city a Democratic fief, the party uses the residents as human shields to avoid acknowledging the results of its control.

Amid the furor over Trump's assessment of Democratic rule in Baltimore, only one local reporter went out to speak to Baltimore residents. Democrats desperately needed to keep the focus on race, not their policies. Trump's truth-telling tweets were the closest the country has ever come to acknowledging the misery that Democratic rule has inflicted on cities across the country.

If the topic at hand is racism, why is it racist to criticize the failures of city leaders in Democratic cities across the country—cities united by high crime, neglect, and Democratic rule? The party that defended Governor Ralph Northam—whose predilection for wearing blackface earned him the nickname "Coonman" in college—thinks criticizing the failures of Democrat policies is racist? Democrats don't want the public's attention diverted to this particular point. Constituents might start asking questions, wondering what they got for their votes. The real racism here is the insistence that black politicians be exempt from criticism because of their race and the assumption that it's permissible to underserve black constituents.

Democrats are brilliant at avoiding responsibility. It's why they are so keen to brand identities: You can't be authentically black unless you're a black Democrat. You can't be authentically Hispanic unless you're a Hispanic Democrat. You can't be an authentically female unless you're a female Democrat. You can't be authentically gay unless you're a gay Democrat. By making these identities their own registered trademarks, Democrats unofficially expand their protected legal status and shield their failed policies from accountability. The problem, as I've heard from many of my listeners across the country, is that many black, Hispanic, female, gay, etc., Americans in cities like Baltimore loudly agree with the criticism of one-party Democratic rule. Some are even rising up and challenging the party—though not necessarily as a Republican, Libertarian, or conservative.

Some think the problem isn't too much involvement by the state but too little, so they challenge their party from the left. Alexandria Ocasio Cortez is the most famous one to do this. A former member of the Democratic Socialists of America, she was open about running as a socialist and a Democrat for the Democrat nomination for her congressional district. She isn't the only one. Some people react to the failure of Democrats' socialist-lite programs by either demanding less government or, in the case of Cortez and the other socialists, demanding more of it.

The Democratic Party is being consumed by the same dirty game it played for so long: The attack-dog socialists whom it used have exerted control, winning more and more influence within both the party and Congress. Democrats still need the socialists to maintain power, but it's a dangerous trade. Going explicitly socialist would doom the Democrats to the dustbin of history. Instead, they're refashioning the party: It believes wealth is evil, government is your church and savior, and independence is selfishness. Virtue is extinct—"virtue signaling" has replaced actual virtue.

What socialists and the social justice warriors propose is forced virtue. But as Milton Friedman pointed out, "forced virtue isn't virtue."[7] What good is the choice between sin and virtue if you lack the freedom to choose? Friedman believed it to be "a meaningless concept." You cannot make a bad society good with force.

You can, however, try to scare people into certain behavior. The left controls the market on violence as a political tactic, most recently seen in the riots of Antifa (an abbreviation of "anti-fascist"—an ironic title if ever there was one). These are groups of well-off white socialists dressed in black who have convinced themselves that they are battling "fascists"—that is, people who don't agree with socialism. College campuses are a favorite place for riots because wealthy white socialist students can behave like brats with impunity. Instead of teaching students how to articulate their views intelligently, we give them "safe spaces" and teach them to scream, set fire to things, assault people, and damage private property if they encounter views they dislike. Antifa is a movement of adult toddlers who never learned the life skill of peacefully coexisting in a diverse society—that is, a society diverse in thought, not just appearance.

American Socialists/Democrats foment political polarization, shaming those on their own side who don't conform to Groupthink. They have long practiced populism—even more so as members of the Democratic Socialists of America such Bernie Sanders and Alexandria Ocasio Cortez have gained influence within the Democratic Party—and have recently taken to comparing themselves to the protesters for liberty in Hong Kong, seemingly unaware of how inapt that comparison is. Socialists protest for *more* government involvement in our everyday lives. Protesters in Hong Kong, are protesting for *less*.

The Socialists/Democrats have built a "cancel culture" in which they try to silence, personally and professionally, anyone who seems to threaten their influence. Apologizing does no good; they will try to destroy you. They "de-platform" those with whom they disagree by convincing Twitter, Facebook, Instagram—even Pinterest—to suspend service to the ideologically unfavored. They have even convinced YouTube to demonetize their opponents' videos.

Socialism supposedly serves the "common good," but what common good emerges from socialist policies? When I saw the trash and derelict structures amid which the good citizens of Baltimore had to live, I suggested on Twitter that MAGA-hatted folks should band together and help Baltimore residents reclaim their neighborhoods from the city's neglect— not as a political stunt, but to show care for one another. That same day the conservative activist Scott Presler, right out of Isaiah 6:8, launched the #CleanUp initiative.[8] He and his volunteers started in Baltimore and removed tons of trash for residents—the elderly unable to do the work themselves and hard-working parents who couldn't afford to take time off of work to do what their elected officials should have done. The #CleanUp crew made two trips to Baltimore and then took their services to places like Los Angeles. Removing fifty tons of garbage from a homeless camp, the volunteers had to wear hazmat suits, facing diseases like typhus and flesh-eating bacteria. Virtually every media outlet ignored it.

When socialists staged an anti–climate change, anti-capitalism, twerking, and confetti party in Washington, D.C., and elsewhere in September 2019, however, they received saturated media coverage. By setting dumpsters on fire (for the environment!) and twerking in denim booty shorts in front of giant climate change banners (twerking for the environment!), the protesters made it clear that exhibitionism, not advocacy, was their real goal. If they cared so much, why didn't *they* volunteer to clean up Baltimore or the homeless camps in L.A.? Perhaps because they needed to form a governing body first and outsource all their stewardship through that entity.

That's the problem with socialism—it likes to outsource neighborly stewardship, which is the responsibility of free men and women. The government is so bloated because it has filled the hole left by people who abandoned their duty to one another—their *voluntary* duty to one another, because being forced to administer care doesn't edify a person the way that voluntary care *does*. God gives free will, but socialist governments do not. When tyrannical governments rob people of their choices in commerce (or speech, or self-preservation), they are stealing the free will God gave them, usurping the place of God, who gives his children the gift of free will with the hope that they will choose his path. No true choice comes from coercion.

I noticed recently that some churches have taken to speaking on social justice, albeit in different ways. But social justice as defined in our culture today is not the justice that Jesus preached. It is state-mandated "equality," which is a departure from the concept originally articulated in Catholic theology, which sought prosperity guided by the free will of the individual in a virtuous society, always taking into account each person's merit based on his effort. Those who believe the state to be morally superior to the will of the individual added the redistribution part. The socialist definition of social justice ignores merit, neuters ambition,

and diminishes the equity of labor. Equal rewards for uneq
unjust and fosters resentment.

Equality is not uniformity. Scripture demands not the equal distribu-
tion of equity unearned by merit ("The one who is unwilling to work
shall not eat"),[9] but rather the equal *shared burden of life* through stewardship of one's fellow man.

The state purports to act on behalf of "the common good." But who
defines the common good? It has long been the justification monstrous
acts by totalitarian governments. What is the good in the common good?
In an era where bad is good and good is bad, how can it be trusted? Who
enforces this arbitrary definition of "common good?" As the great theo-
logian of the free market Michael Novak wrote,

> A central misuse of the term "common good" became clear to
> me for the first time when, at the Human Rights Commission
> in Bern, I was prodding the Soviet delegation to recognize the
> right of married couples, one of whose partners was from one
> nation, the other from another, to share residence in whichever
> nation they chose. The Soviets staunchly resisted—in the name
> of the common good. The Soviet Union, they insisted, had
> invested great sums of money and much effort in giving an
> education to each Soviet citizen. The common good, they said,
> demands that these citizens now make comparable contribu-
> tions in return. Therefore, the Soviet partner could not leave.
> Individual desires must bow to the common good of all.
>
> In this way, the common good becomes an excuse for total
> state control. That was the excuse on which totalitarianism
> was built. You can achieve the common good better if there
> is a total authority, and you must then limit the desires and
> wishfulness of individuals.[10]

An appeal to "the common good" is an excuse for tyranny. I'd go so
far as to argue that faith is freedom, the opposite of the restrictions that

tyrannical regimes impose on their citizens. That is why the Founders, who would enshrine our individual rights in the Constitution, noted in the Declaration of Independence that they come from God. An atheist would be less free were his rights subject to the whims of man rather than predicated on the "laws of nature and of nature's God" because man is corrupt and sinful. Does anybody trust to the judgment of man something as supremely important as his natural rights?

As I said earlier, racism is a sin. Sexism is a sin. The act or thought of holding hatred in one's heart toward a son or daughter of God is a sin. Sin is hated, not people. The command God gives most frequently in the Bible is to love one another. Behavior that is in disobedience of this command is sinful and sits in judgment of God's will.

Social justice warriors are correct about one thing: Some people are born with or into certain privileges while others are not. Some people are born into the picture-perfect family with two parents, siblings, a dog, a house, and a reliable, structured home life. Others are born into situations of abuse—substance abuse, sexual abuse, physical abuse. Still others are born to single mothers who struggle to pay the bills. I wasn't born into privilege: I was born into a volatile situation and ended up with a poor single mother whose rural high school education barely prepared her for the life she needed to lead to raise her daughter. My "privilege" as a child was having a meal of milk gravy and biscuits while my mother went hungry. My "privilege" was being good at sports but never having a single person in the stands to see me.

Some people are born into money, some people are born into happy homes. Some aren't born into families at all; they *make* families when adopted by eager parents who are unable to conceive. Some people are privileged enough to be citizens of the United States, while others suffer under the cruelty of tyrants. Some people aren't privileged enough to be born at all, their lives ended because they are inconvenient.

There is *privilege* and there is *advantage*. We work to ensure that our children have the best *advantage* in life by educating them, nurturing their spiritual and physical growth. There has never been a time in which all persons were born with equal advantages. To acknowledge that is not a sign of prejudice, but it is prejudice to assign fault to people for decisions their ancestors made.

Demanding equality in every respect denies the unique and God-given talents of the individual. We are burdening people with a new original sin while ignoring that environment is more powerful than "privilege." The one privilege in which we *are* equal is the ability to overcome our environment. Were you raised in a healthy culture with a perfect family and no worries about making ends meet? I wasn't. And yet I overcame it. I'm certainly not the only one, nor the worst-case scenario by far.

Multitudes of people are living evidence of the power of will over environment. Our nation's first black president, for example, was born into more privilege than many, while Alexander Hamilton, one of the most influential Founding Fathers, was born out of wedlock and orphaned as a child. Too many focus on their struggle to the exclusion of their very real gifts and advantages. This isn't to say that unfairness doesn't exist—it does because human beings are compromised, sinful creatures.

Those who have been blessed with advantages are called by God to bless others on his behalf. Stewardship cannot be left to a godless government to perform. It has to be the joyful act of grateful people who know where their blessings come from and are eager to show their appreciation by sharing where they see a need. They are to be God's hands and feet for others. Jesus admonishes us, "But the one who does not know and does things deserving punishment will be beaten with few blows. From everyone who has been given much, much will be demanded; and from the one who has been entrusted with much, much more will be asked (Luke 12:48).

The Parable of the Talents in the Gospel of Matthew (25:14–30) illustrates this principle. Many of you know the story well. A man going on a journey entrusted his property to three of his servants, each according to his ability. To the first servant he gave five talents, to the second he gave two, and to the third servant he gave one. While their master was gone, the first servant traded with his five talents, making five more. The second servant likewise doubled his two talents. The third servant buried his one talent in the ground. When the master returned from his journey, he settled accounts with each of the servants. To the first he said, "Well done, good and faithful servant. You have been faithful over a little; I will set you over much. Enter into the joy of your master." He said the same to the second servant. But he scolded the third servant, taking his one talent and giving it to the first servant. The parable concludes, "For to everyone who has will more be given, and he will have an abundance. But from the one who has not, even what he has will be taken away."

Each person is called to use his gifts—which are entrusted to him by God—to benefit those in need. God isn't calling you to outsource your stewardship to the government. For people of faith, this was never more evident than in 2 Corinthians 9:7. Paul writes: *"Let each one give as he purposes in his heart, not grudgingly or of necessity; for God loves a cheerful giver"*

There are two truths that carry all of Biblical law: those who run a socialist system are the gods, and when you replace God you replace grace.

We cannot be complacent in the service of others and withhold our stewardship—we've seen the failure of government to fulfill the role best left to the compassionate stewardship of individuals (for example, entitlement programs), and government stewardship is abysmal. One of the reasons I am so vehemently against nationalized health care is because of what I saw firsthand with Veterans Affairs when my Grandpa took ill. Some have had wonderful experiences with the VA, but those stories I've found are the exception not the rule. One inspector general report found that over 300,000 veterans may have died while waiting for their VA care. Thanks to the 24-7 dutiful attention of his family and their persistent contact with the VA, my grandfather was in good hands. I once overhead my mother on the phone with one of her siblings, discussing how the VA had denied a hearing aid for Grandpa because he was elderly and thus not a "cost-effective" candidate. My mother, her siblings, myself and my cousins certainly didn't look at him as not being cost-effective. There isn't much that will get you over hearing how a bureaucratic agency has reduced the life of your amazing, selfless, World War II veteran grandfather with over twenty-three grandchildren who adored him, respected by his community, to a simple "not cost effective" classification. This is where government stewardship gets you and why I oppose it (it's also why several years ago I chose to support an organization that assists veterans and help whenever my ability allows).

The failure of individual stewardship created an opening for government exploitation. Christians believe that God is the God of all grace, and when God is removed from mainstream culture, the incentive to be a just and forgiving people evaporates. When you know you've been forgiven much, you yourself find it easier to forgive others. When people have been generous with you, you find it easier to be generous in return. Bernie Sanders once proclaimed[11] at a political fundraiser: "I don't believe in charities. The *New York Times* noted at the time: "The Mayor, who is a Socialist, went on to question the "fundamental concepts on which charities are based" and contended that government, rather than charity organizations, should take over responsibility for social programs."

Sanders, ever the socialist, has kept true to his word, hardly donating anything to charity[12]—particularly in the years he made a million dollars or more (despite having no discernible skills outside of the government sector and never having held a private sector job). Socialists like Sanders outsource their responsibility for stewardship because they're too lazy or greedy to do it themselves. It certainly can't be because they're convinced the government does a better job than the people themselves—an idea unsupported by any real data.[13] Socialists have no faith in the private individual because they worship the god of government. Christians, mostly Republicans and conservatives, have no faith in government but worship the God of grace who calls his kingdom to be his hands and feet, and from their abilities bless those in need. Even libertarians, which I sometimes facetiously refer to as Republicans/conservatives-without-God in front of my Libertarian friends, possess a healthy suspicion of government promising to do what people can do for themselves. Socialists believe that wealth redistribution through confiscatory financial schemes—the spoils of which are mostly sucked up by bureaucracy—serves others best. James 2:15-18 addresses the issue of private stewardship of those less fortunate: "In the same way, faith by itself, if it is not accompanied by action, is dead. But someone will say, 'You have faith; I have deeds.' Show me your faith without deeds and I will show you my faith by my deeds."

A government that claims to care for the poor, the downtrodden, the champion-less provides some meager support, then pockets the rest or spends it on items that court votes for the next election. God does not abide selfishness, and Luke 12:48 makes this abundantly clear: "From everyone who has been given much, much will be demanded; and from the one who has been entrusted with much, much more will be asked."

We are called to minister to those in need for our own spiritual edification. Proverbs 3:27 says, "Do not withhold good from those to whom it is due when it is in your power to act."

I think some support the export of their stewardship to the government because they trust the government more than they trust themselves. Others export their stewardship because they are too lazy to do it themselves. The *Washington Examiner*[14] brilliantly captured it: "Socialism is the enemy of charity because it outsources all compassion and altruism to the state."

Out of sight, out of mind, they may think— an overarching theme throughout socialism and communism (and one is just a stepping-stone to the other). Socialists like to play Santa Claus while the taxpayers play the part of the elves. Identity politics reduces the person to a singular issue and distances us not only from the merits of an issue, but from the humanity of those involved in the discussion. They want grace, but "grace" on their terms. They want to erode ambition and replace it with their "grace," social welfare. Big government grows bigger by replacing individuals' ambition. What need is there for personal ambition if government will provide, albeit it meagerly, for all your needs from cradle to grave? Free* college! Free* healthcare! All in the name of equality! And if you don't consent to paying for these free* things, then you are selfish and support inequality. If statists define selfishness in this regard as "being stingy," then how to define the lusting after another's money for things one can afford oneself? What room is there for motivation or ambition, if its incentive is already federally fulfilled? As I said earlier, "equality" as defined by statists and socialists, demands that we disregard merit when making decisions about people and equity. This removal of merit from the conversation removes the incentive for ambition, unfairly diminishing the value of labor. What charity is this? How is this mercy? Specifically—how is the meager promise of a mediocre government allowance in any way a merciful evaluation of a human's potential?

Ask yourself: Do you *truly* trust your government to be steward to the less fortunate and to properly attend to their needs? Was the government successful in doing this through the Veterans' Administration? An inspector general report[15] stated that government incompetency in the VA may have cost over 307,000 veteran lives.

"I am for doing good to the poor," Ben Franklin once opined, "but I differ in opinion of the means. I think the best way of doing good to the poor, is not making them easy in poverty, but leading or driving them out of it." What of your tax dollars? Do you trust a government that spent over $2 billion[16] on a clunky, mostly inoperable health care website to wisely spend your dollars? Do you trust them with to "save" your money for social security, a program which promised older generations that it would be there for them when they needed it? Now the headlines announce its insolvency within sixteen years.[17]

Some maintain they haven't the time to be stewards of their community, to volunteer, to foster, even to be involved locally at all. Said Thomas Jefferson of the responsibilities ushered by freedom: "I would rather be exposed to the inconveniences attending too much liberty than those attending too small a degree of it."

There is nothing that can replace the human touch in attending to human needs. Nothing fills faceless statistics out into real people like meeting them where they are. Even God meets us where we are. For example: it's easy to write off the poor, unwed mom in whose ear agencies like Planned Parenthood whisper sweet, poisonous promises of an easier life without the "burden" (as a former president once said) of a baby. It's easy to deny her grace, look down our noses, and lament that she's simply suffering the consequences of her own choices. She may be. That may be true. It may even be easy to say that if you don't believe in a redemptive path. But what if her path to redemption is through you? Who is standing in the gap for her? The taxpayer-funded agency whose idea of grace is one fewer life? You can't blame her for considering an abortion; it sounds easier than the endless hours of work, worry, and guilt wondering if she'll ever be good enough for her child. Society tells her she's not strong enough to handle a child, while also peppering her with withering social guilt. You be the person to tell her she *is* strong enough. Instead of turning a blind eye or merely sending a check for pro-life advocacy, meet her where she is, stand in the gap for her. She needs babysitting while she works; volunteer for it yourself, or if you've the means, hire one for her. She needs a crib? Get one for her. While blessings come from God, they so very, very often come *through* other people. Even if you're not a person of faith, are you too good to stand in the gap for someone else? I'm not talking about lifelong, privatized welfare, I'm talking about temporary, private stewardship while someone gets back on their feet. The accusation that this is simply privatized welfare springs from the exact attitude that calls Christians and conservatives callous and punitive. It's a hypocritical, legalistic viewpoint that denies grace. You trust that such unique, individualized attention can be achieved many times over by the same government that wasted 55 billion taxpayer dollars[18] on implementing a new healthcare policy? Now, there are *some* good people *within* agencies who do an amazing job within the limits of their ability to care for people, but wouldn't it be better to remove the excuse of government outsourcing and meet these needs ourselves? Are people so lacking in confidence in their own abilities, or their ability to inspire others to do the same, that they can't leave the feeding tube of government?

This is why we are called to steward, and this is also why steward-ship must be voluntary. How can you measure the change in a person's heart if the only change is made by force?

I firmly believe that were it not for the charity of faithful Christians our world would be unrecognizable. Christians do and have done so much good in the world and to so many. I myself have felt spiritually challenged by the example others have set. Checkbook ministry is great—there are many amazing works funded by very generous people. But ministry person-to-person, as we've seen not just in the United States but around the world, bears the most fruit, and it doesn't require wealth in anything but love to make it happen. It's not a calling limited *just to Christians*, nor are these ideals limited to people of faith. You don't have to accept Jesus as your Savior to recognize that ongoing, voluntary assistance of citizens is superior to the clinical, poorly run administration of government. It's easy to spend money, as the government as shown. Is not the willingness to spend your own *time* in this effort a declaration of love for your fellow man? Is this not a more complete understanding of grace?

"Chick-fil-A Is Growing So Fast It Could Surpass Starbucks," read one recent headline.[19] The fast-food chain is the third largest restaurant chain[20] and is poised to topple McDonald's with no signs of slowing.[21] Chick-fil-A makes more per restaurant than McDonald's, Starbucks, and Subway *combined*.[22] America loves eating at Chick-fil-A, despite how the news says Dan Cathy is a bad, bad man who hates the gays and gives money to despotic entities like Iran, which kills people for being gay—oh wait, Cathy didn't give them money, that was the United States government during the Obama administration.

Why is Chick-fil-A so popular? Obviously it's because of their chicken—particularly the spicy chicken sandwich, which is the valedictorian of the other chicken sandwiches—but there's something else. In 2018[23] the American Customer Satisfaction Index's Restaurant Report surveyed over 22,000 people, and Chick-fil-A beat out all the rest to take first place for their "superior" customer service. Dan Cathy, CEO of the family business, has said:[24]

> Every life has a story, and often our customers and our employees, need a little grace and a little space when you deal with them because they are either experiencing a problem, just finished having a problem, or are about to have one. The word 'restaurant' means place of restoration, and we think of Chick-fil-A as an oasis where people can be restored. We strive to treat people better than the place down the street. One way we do that is by remembering that we're all people with a lot of emotional things going on that don't necessarily show on the surface, so we try to offer amenities and kindness that minister to the heart.

Cathy also cited Matthew 5:41: "If anyone forces you to go one mile, go with them two miles." Cathy understands that leaders serve the most. The man who has said, "putting people before profits is how we've tried to operate from the beginning," didn't need the government to tell him to do this. His family-run business does it because they truly value the people they serve, including their employees. Like his father, Truett Cathy, before him, he knows you care for the people who care for you; it's good business—but more important than being "good business," it's the right way to treat people. To this end, Chick-fil-A has a scholarship program for its employees and offers them access to tuition discounts.[25] *Money Magazine* ranked the fast-food company[26] first for its 401(k) plan, which is triple the standard in the industry, and the business was the only one from the restaurant sector to make top ten for "Best Places to Work."[27] We give Chick-fil-A our money willingly, and they work better than the U.S. government, which takes our money against our will for service nowhere near Chick-fil-A's level. Chick-fil-A cares for its customers, and you know this because they care for their employees. Cathy ensures his employees are made to feel valued and like the company emphasizes with them. Cathy works at his restaurants regularly, on the floor just like any other member of his team, so he knows exactly what his employees deal with daily. Socialists, instead of raging at Cathy for his privately held beliefs, which have not prevented his service, stewardship, or hiring, ought to copy his business plan going forward: be a good and trusted steward in all things.

CHAPTER THREE

The Death of Nuance

"Tyranny is the deliberate removal of nuance."

—Albert Maysles

Impulse, not intellectualism, is what drives outrage today. Someone said something wrong, and everyone knows that the number one rule of the Internet is that people with wrong opinions cannot be left alone with all those wrong opinions. But what if they turn out to be right? What happens if you hear their side of the story and find yourself in agreement with a couple aspects of it—not all of it, perhaps, but they make a couple of good points. Many dislike doing this for two reasons. First, indulging an opposing viewpoint costs something. No one wants to expend the effort on so risky an enterprise. It's easier to close your eyes, buckle up, and go with the flow. Second, conceding that someone with whom you disagree might have a good-faith interest in reaching the truth requires grace. Most of us are too busy nursing bruised egos and grudges to give someone else that kind of credit.

People have lost the ability to think in various shades of gray. It's either-or. No nuance, nothing to trigger the performance of reason. Thoughtful analysis of potential solutions is often boring, it's not theatrical, and it challenges the reader/listener/viewer to reexamine his reasons for supporting a particular position and to consider the alternatives—not

39

necessarily to modify his own principles, but to appeal to those whose concerns are going unattended. The binary tribalism of our politics chokes off deeper discussion and prevents the discovery of common ground.

Tribalism deals in absolutes.

Nuance cannot exist where binary tribalism dominates.

This is where our culture finds itself—and sadly, it is rewarded behavior. Speeches, columns, tweets, posts that adopt absolutism are simultaneously the most controversial and the most popular. Red-meat platitudes win cheers but do little to advance the debate.

If you champion plan A then you oppose plan B, while if you champion plan B you oppose plan A. You're not allowed to like parts of both plan A and B or even to listen to plan B's advocates long enough to respond to their concerns. Binary tribalism also gives way to purposeful mischaracterization, a favorite ploy of the far left to shoot down their ideological opposition without the hard work of substantiating their accusations or provide supporting evidence for their arguments. It's insidious and heavily relied upon by those who wish to impugn their opponents as hateful or bigoted.

An example: One day in 2017, at the end of my daily TV program on NRATV, I commented on the news that Mattel was attempting to make the children's show *Thomas and Friends* more diverse by adding "female" trains and trains of color to the lineup. Noting the ever-increasing reach of the social justice warrior mentality, which finds cause for offense in everything, I asked how anyone could consider Thomas the Tank Engine racist. As I asked the question, an absurd image of the *Thomas and Friends* trains sporting Ku Klux Klan hoods briefly appeared on screen. "Oh. That's why!" I said with mock dismay. "They have a point about the trains, then, yes. I agree." The point, obviously, was to poke fun at the social justice warriors, who think there's a Klansman under every bed.

Media Matters, the leftist "watchdog" organization "dedicated to comprehensively monitoring, analyzing, and correcting conservative

misinformation in the U.S. media," breathlessly reported that NRATV
had featured *Thomas and Friends* characters in KKK hoods, utterly
ignoring the satire. The legacy media began repeating the propaganda,
as Media Matters intended, even trying to drag Mattel and Thomas the
Tank's creator into the manufactured controversy. The moronic and
intentionally misleading reporting convinced me that nuance is dead. I
was tempted to swear off jokes, leaving them to the comedians, but not
even comedy is safe anymore.

Nuance is dead! Long live ... mindless literalism! Unless you're a
Democrat in blackface.

There was a time in our modern political history when we could have
in-depth discussions, but nowadays people are too eager to score a "got-
cha!" Long-form discussion invites leftists to search for comments that
can be stripped of context and presented in a misleading way. It's a shallow, vain, and evil game that progressives and a few "conservatives"
enjoy because it saves them the hard work of making better arguments
on their own. People who care about arriving at the truth don't do this.
They aren't interested in simply winning a debate; they're interested in
doing right by the issue on which the debate is held.

In October 2015, Yale administrators issued a campus-wide email
from the Intercultural Affairs Committee that encouraged students to
avoid Halloween costumes that appropriated other cultures, offering a
checklist to determine if a costume was offensive. The Puritans, it was
clear, were alive and well at Yale. Ericka Christakis, a childhood development expert at the university, responded to the email from the perspective
of a professional who believes that adults' constant coddling of young
people inculcates unrealistic expectations about the world:

> I don't wish to trivialize genuine concerns about cultural and
> personal representation, and other challenges to our lived
> experience in a plural community. I know that many decent
> people have proposed guidelines on Halloween costumes
> from a spirit of avoiding hurt and offense. I laud those goals,

in theory, as most of us do. But in practice, I wonder if we should reflect more transparently, as a community, on the consequences of an institutional (which is to say: bureaucratic and administrative) exercise of implied control over college students....

Even if we could agree on how to avoid offense—and I'll note that no one around campus seems overly concerned about the offense taken by religiously conservative folks to skin-revealing costumes—I wonder, and I am not trying to be provocative: Is there no room anymore for a child or young person to be a little bit obnoxious ... a little bit inappropriate or provocative or, yes, offensive? American universities were once a safe space not only for maturation but also for a certain regressive, or even transgressive, experience; increasingly, it seems, they have become places of censure and prohibition. And the censure and prohibition come from above, not from yourselves! Are we all okay with this transfer of power? Have we lost faith in young people's capacity—in your capacity—to exercise self-censure, through social norming, and also in your capacity to ignore or reject things that trouble you?

Referring to her husband, also a Yale professor, Christakis added, "Nicholas says, if you don't like a costume someone is wearing, look away, or tell them you are offended. Talk to each other. Free speech and the ability to tolerate offence are the hallmarks of a free and open society."

Her questions should have launched a wider conversation on maturity, self-sovereignty, appreciation vs. appropriation, etc., but they didn't. There can be no questions, no discussion, no nuance—Christakis had questioned the Intercultural Affairs Committee. Proving her point, a campus rage mob descended on her husband. The Christakises resigned their positions as faculty-in-residence. (Nicholas maintains his tenured position.)

Baseball may be America's pastime, but outrage is its new hobby. Outrage—it's all the rage! Politics can be categorized as BT or AT—before

Trump or after Trump. Democrats, and our political and cultural discussion in general, have become excruciatingly more literal since 2016.

Today's political discourse goes something like this: If, during a conversation about breakfast items, you were to say, "I really enjoy pancakes for breakfast," the response would be "WHY DO YOU HATE WAFFLES?"

"Well, I don't hate waffles, I just prefer pancakes," you might reply.

"But that excludes waffles," the SJW would counter.

"Well, I prefer pancakes over waffles, but I don't hate waffles," would be a sufficient response.

"See, I knew it. You hate waffles," would come the response. "You can't just say that you like pancakes better and assume that everyone knows you don't mean that you also hate waffles."

Well, yes, that's exactly what you or I or any grown-up would do. We would assume that the person to whom we were replying had enough sense and courtesy to realize that the approval of one thing doesn't entail the denigration of another. But this response requires that you don't assume the worst about the person to whom you're speaking.

This is how desperate partisan politics has now become. Nuance is now provocative. Nuance is now risky.

For instance, if you support the Second Amendment and would like to keep or carry a firearm for your own protection or the protection of your loved ones, you'll be accused of supporting mass shootings. Why would anyone say such a thing and ignore the legitimate reasons a law-abiding person would have for his position? Some people have experienced trauma that has compelled them to seek out ways to prevent it from occurring again. Others are simply afraid of becoming victims themselves. The reasons for owning a gun are ignored because it's easier to smear your opponent as an unfeeling murderer. I carry to prevent myself from becoming a victim of violence. I carry because I love life—not just mine and my family's, but all innocent life. I, and plenty of others like me, care so much that we work at honing skills we never want to use. But to consider this side of the discussion, one must consider the other side. It isn't easy to tell a person who has no experience with fire-arms to go get a gun if he wants to protect himself.

A friend who was born and raised in New York City once told me that his family let him ride the subway alone when he was ten years old. I was floored. He laughed and said that it was normal where he was from, and no one thought anything of it. Yet when this friend accompanied my family to the range for the first time, he couldn't believe that some fami-lies were teaching children as young as eight or ten how to shoot and responsibly handle guns.

Political tribalism hasn't just divided the right and left. It has also provoked chaos within the Democratic and Republican parties. Repub-licans grapple with the "Never Trumpers," who cannot bring themselves to support Trump, even if he is advancing their social and economic causes. Giving any credit given to Trump, in their view, is to acquiesce to immorality and the destruction of the GOP. On the flip side, you have an element within the GOP who are so fervently pro-Trump that they refuse to criticize any decision or policy. These factions hate each other, spending an inordinate amount of time on social media trying to influ-ence the people in the middle. Both sides actually agree with each other on most issues, including their view of the executive as bigger than the mission of governing America.

Democrats have enjoyed the GOP civil war because it has enabled them to keep their struggles in the shadows. The Democratic Party is now socialist in all but name. For several years, stalwarts like Nancy Pelosi used the far left as a Get Out the Vote army while denying them greater influence in the party. That dynamic changed in 2016, and the old guard has been trying to claw back its influence. The socialists within the party have made it clear that pro-life Democrats are unwelcome, Representative Pramila Jayapal telling the press last spring,

> Personally, I do think there should be a core set of Demo-cratic ideals that we all agree to.... You can't say you're a Democrat if you're against immigrants, if you're against

abortion, if you're against gay marriage and LGBTQ rights. I'm not sure what it means to be. Democrat if all of those things are true.

Social issues, the fight over how quickly to descend into the socialist nightmare of single-payer health insurance, and certain positions on foreign policy have driven a wedge between the far left and more moderate elements of the Democratic Party.

When nuance died it took common sense with it. For example, in September 2019, I came across a news report from California titled "Fremont Police Tesla Near-Dead Battery Forces Officer Off Pursuit."[1] Someone had forgotten to recharge the battery of a Tesla patrol car, and the policeman driving it had to abandon a chase. (Other officers were able to take over the pursuit.) After reading the story over the air and tweeting about it, I gave it no more thought until Elon Musk replied the next day, "Media report was false."[2]

I was puzzled. I checked the news story, and nothing had been changed. Then I learned that there is a Tesla fan club on social media, some of whose members had had a fit. In the span of an afternoon, the story had turned into "a thing." Other reporters got involved,[3] the Fremont police issued another statement,[4] and a tidal wave of outrage washed over my Twitter account. These are a few of the milder ones that don't refer to me as words you can't say on TV, radio, in front of polite company, or in church:

> "Same people quick to yell fake news cling to it when it fits their narrative. Dana Loesch is a partisan shill. What's new."[5]
>
> "what was the purpose of your retweet? You read the title and decided it's true enough for you to show your followers? This is why cake [sic] news is a thing."[6]
>
> "So you just deliberately spread falsehoods and when found to be false you double up?!"[7]
>
> "why retweet something that was wrong and not correct it?"[8]

I'm not sure what that fellow meant by "doubling up." People also demanded I edit and clarify the story I didn't write, for the media outlet I did not work for. No one wanted to slow down the dial-up to eleven long enough to process the story. I tried explaining to the mob that I did not have the authority to edit this outlet's stories, but that changed no one's mind. None of the people raging had even read the story but assumed it was all about smearing Tesla. The first paragraph of the story explained that the incident was the result of user error—someone forgot to recharge the battery. But this Twitter mob assumed that this was a hit piece, and because I shared it I must have been responsible for it. Someone pointedly asked if I would think the story was still funny if it had been a gas-powered car, and I answered truthfully that yes, I would. But who can miss the humor in this story about a city so determined to go green that it purchases very expensive Tesla police cars that poop out in a chase. Even if you wear Birkenstocks, use crystals, make your clothes out of hemp, and eat vegan cheese, it's funny. I worry for the poor souls who can't find the humor in that because they're too busy raging at everything in life.

"Outrage is a commodity," noted Todd Phillips, the director of the 2019 film *Joker*, when asked about the social justice warriors accusing him of glorifying violence in his movie about a comic book character.[9] Before the movie was even released, several social justice warriors insisted that it was going to inspire a bunch of white "involuntary celibates" (called "incels" by people who have spent five figures on a gender-studies degree only to end up bagging groceries and writing missives on movies they haven't seen for miles-wide-inches-deep culture sites) to commit acts of violence. No one has any idea why this thought occurred to them, but alas, "outrage is a commodity."

Phillips explained to *The Wrap* that he wasn't trying "to push buttons" but wanted to make a "real movie ... under the guise of a comic book film." He wanted to create an origin story that answered the question "How do screwed-up people get screwed up?"—a timely question concerning young men these days. Heather Antos, a comic-book editor, disapproved of even having the conversation about this film:

I don't want to watch a man get rejected by women as an excuse for his future of domestic abuse.

I don't want to be shown what a poor, unfortunate underdog this man was who was sadly forced by circumstances and that nasty Batman to take up a life of crime.

I don't want to have sympathy for a man best known for his robbery, murder, and arguable rape shoved down my throat for two hours.

I don't want this to be sold as a relatable story that can happen to anyone with a bad enough day, and I don't want to be around any of the lonely white boys who relate to it....

I don't know if there ever is a good time for a movie that paints mass murder as the logical conclusion of a socially isolated, debatably neurodivergent white man being failed by the system....[10]

Apparently it didn't occur to her not to see the movie. She says the movie is "problematic," but what she complains about are simply reasons she doesn't like the film; they don't make the film "problematic" for everyone else. A reviewer at Comic Book Resource explains that *Joker* is "a cautionary tale to rational viewers. No rational person would be motivated by watching the film to commit crimes."[11]

The reviewer Richard Lawson thinks Phillips wants viewers "in some way" to sympathize with Arthur Fleck, the tormented young man who becomes the Joker.[12] I disagree. Sympathy may well be Lawson's own reaction to the slow, agonizing shaping of Fleck into the Joker and the recognition that even monsters begin as human beings. Lawson may not be sympathizing with Fleck as much as he's mourning the death of whatever remnant of humanity Fleck had left. He's mourning what may be Fleck's only chance of redemption.

Lawson also thinks the Joker "certainly is political." I don't believe any new politics has been introduced—it's just "eat the rich." The rich are responsible for all the ills of society. Not the people who make their money in the shadows through extortion—the crooked cops, the gang-sters. We may revile them, but the people of Gotham blame the Wayne family.

Variety's Owen Gleiberman adds:

> Of course, a rebellion against the ruling elite—which is what Arthur's vigilante action comes to symbolize—is more plau-sible now than it was a decade ago. "Joker" is a comic-book tale rendered with sinister topical fervor. When Arthur, on the elevator, connects with Sophie (Zazie Beetz), his neigh-bor, the two take turns miming Travis Bickle's finger-gun-against-the-head suicide gesture, which becomes the film's key motif. It's a way of saying: This is what America has come to—a place where people feel like blowing their brains out....
>
> And when he gets his fluky big shot to go on TV, we think we know what's going to happen (that he's destined to be humiliated), but what we see, instead, is a monster reborn with a smile. And lo and behold, we're on his side. Because the movie does something that flirts with danger—it gives evil a clown-mask makeover, turning it into the sickest pos-sible form of cool.[13]

Not America—but definitely Gotham. Since childhood I've never regarded Gotham as anything other than a corrupt hellscape—East St. Louis writ large. I always wondered why no one ever left. I chuckled at Gleiberman's "clown-mask makeover" because I'm not sure a clown mask would be an improvement. If anything, it's more sinister. Again, you're not on Fleck's side in the sense Gleiberman suggests. You're grasp-ing for anything to stop Fleck's descent into irredeemable evil. This is important: Phillips is not glorifying the evil that Fleck becomes, he is showing you how it happens.

There's a real conversation that was missed here.

Note how Gleiberman, Lawson, and even the CBR.com writer approached *Joker*—first, they saw the film, and second, they were willing to dive deeper. Antos's aversion seems purely visceral and sexist.

Have we not already had such a character in Norman Bates? Is this not, in its basest form, the retelling of the unsociable, demented man who lives with his mother in the classic *Pyscho*? Good grief, *Friday the 13th* has a similar storyline with the relationship of its protagonist, Jason, his mother, and his childhood. Are we now to find fault with every decent film, ignoring the nuances of the characters, and go with whatever social headline is trending as a way to satisfy the desire for outrage?

Instead of discussing how the movie sheds light on a newly-defined and exaggerated subculture, we are flirting with modern-day book burning—but with film. A big question that no one has touched: If there is such a concern over a subculture of young men, what about our society as a whole? What about our hurried lives, our dereliction of stewardship? What about the endless hours we spend fraternizing online as opposed to real life, the nastiness of the cancel culture and the outrage mobs? Do we fail to see the solutions to these problems because of our own apathy?

Why are we afraid to have these complex and nuanced discussions? Why are we afraid to own our contribution to this problem? Because no one wants to be indicted by his own apathy. Why must everything descend into shallow outrage—particularly before people even know what they're discussing?

Our binary tribalism is at its worst in the debate on immigration.

Much of the conversation about immigration disingenuously fails to distinguish those who enter the country illegally from those who enter legally. Because Republicans oppose *illegal* immigration, Democrats have taken to accusing Republicans of opposing *all* immigration. This charge, which simply isn't true, ignores the complexity of the issue.

Some Republicans have also expressed concern about the number of immigrants legally entering the United States, asking whether it is proportional to our available resources, including economic opportunity.

Democrats call this line of thinking "racist," but race isn't a component—and it's an odd accusation to make considering the number of minority Americans in our country who also share these concerns.

With Democrats, it's "either-or" when it comes to immigration. You are either for decriminalizing illegal entry and opening the borders, or you're a racist. They play the identity politics card because they have no rational answer to Republicans' concerns.

At the same time, some Republicans view concern for the children trafficked at the border, some of whom have been separated from their families because of an Obama-era policy, as being soft on illegal entry or even amnesty. This take is just as disingenuous and logically flawed as Democrats' arguments. You can feel for those fleeing corrupt government or conflict and yet still support an orderly manner of dealing with the problem. You can support legal immigration and simultaneously support a system that balances the number of persons entering legally with our ability to handle them.

One of the left's favorite rhetorical tactics is deploying children as human shields against criticism. In the gun control debate, teenagers—some of them legal adults—will make horrible accusations. If you question them, you will be attacked by the rage mob for meanly arguing with children. Nothing was ever said of the adults actually using children as a shield behind which they launched incendiary personal attacks against their ideological opposition.

The first time I appeared on CNN's *New Day*, the host, Alisyn Camerota, noted that I had said—accurately, by the way—that "many in legacy media love mass shootings" because of the ratings they generate. When Camerota said my words were "malicious," I pointed out that she had let people, without correction, accuse me and other law-abiding gun-owners of being child-murderers. A case in point was David Hogg, the high school gun-control activist who had made that slur explicitly on Camerota's show.[14]

The tactic of using children as shields was in play again when the Swedish teenaged climate-change activist Greta Thunberg was elevated from protesting solo in front of her parliament building to speaking at the United Nations. In a speech to members of Congress,[15] she scolded the country leading the way[16] for the reduction of CO2 emissions. (I'm not sure if she met with anyone from China regarding that country's emissions.)[17] It's easier to send out the children than to worry about the consequences of your bad arguments. Kids' illogical and unsupported claims are more easily accepted because they're kids. But if someone challenges the premise, the rage mob reach for their pitchforks.

Another tactic progressives use is claiming that the existence of some-one who believes differently from them makes them feel "unsafe." In July 2019, six Arizona police officers were asked to leave a Starbucks because a customer complained that their presence made them feel "unsafe."[18] That same month in that same state a man admitted to killing a black teenager because the teenager's choice of music made him feel "unsafe."[19] Branding completely innocuous things or people as "unsafe" can be wrongly used to justify everything from censorship to murder. There is no discussion; it's *unsafe*. The real danger is thinking that ideas are dangerous.

This new principle of absolutes, or Sith Logic ("Only the Sith think in absolutes," Yoda once advised), was on display in the days following the savage beating of the reporter Andy Ngo by the very fascist Antifa. Numerous media outlets identified the self-described left-of-center reporter as a "conservative" because he did not put a favorable spin on their destruction. Ngo may be gay and the son of immigrants, but he isn't the right kind of journalist. The same thing happens to any gay, black, Hispanic, transgender, or other minority who criticizes the left's actions. Don't think you're safe if you play neutral. Ngo was neutral toward Antifa, allowing its actions to speak for themselves.

The enemy of binary tribalism is common ground, and rediscovering the nuance of national discourse is the first step in establishing it. If you agree with one aspect of an ideology but not the rest, you risk coming to a better understanding of the political opposition. You might even see them as human.

Common ground is not allowed.

CHAPTER FOUR

The History of Leftist Violence

"No mercy for these enemies of the people, the enemies of socialism, the enemies of the working people! War to the death against the rich and their hangers-on, the bourgeois intellectuals; war on the rogues, the idlers, and the rowdies!"

— *Vladimir Lenin*

The summer of 2019 began with a bang—literally. Willem Van Spronsen was killed by police as he tried to blow up an Immigration and Customs Enforcement detention center in Tacoma, Washington. He left behind a manifesto that referred to the center as a "concentration camp," an appellation popularized by numerous elected Democrats, particularly Alexandria Ocasio-Cortez. From the *New York Times*: "'This administration has established concentration camps on the southern border of the United States for immigrants, where they are being brutalized with dehumanizing conditions and dying,' Ms. Ocasio-Cortez wrote on Twitter, amplifying comments she had made on her Instagram feed on Monday night."[1]

She also tweeted of a video of herself at a detention center: "I flew to the concentration camp where the Trump admin was keeping children they stole from their parents."[2] The detention policy she attributes to Trump was instituted by President Bill Clinton[3] and expanded by President Obama.[4] It is often unclear whether Ocasio-Cortez understands in the slightest whatever law or policy she is talking about, but she had people believing that the Trump administration was running concentration camps.

To celebrate the last day of Pride Month 2019, violent Antifa rioters in Portland robbed and beat a *Quillette* reporter in the streets, sending him to the hospital with a brain bleed.[5] But let me rephrase that with appropriate intersectional sensitivity—violent Antifa rioters in Portland robbed and beat a *gay reporter who is the son of Vietnamese immigrants.* Andy Ngo has long covered Antifa protests/riots, simply letting his camera roll as they harass and bully drivers, throw rocks at people, and beat the elderly with crowbars. They don't come off well in Ngo's reporting, and they resent it.

Members of Antifa purport to be *protesting* fascism, but the videos of their attacks on other people for simply existing give the impression that they're *practicing* it instead. The Portland chapter looks like it got lost on the way to an underground rave and instead stumbled into a military surplus store. The Portland police are nowhere to be seen in most of these videos, particularly the ones in which these valiant anti-fascists are punching cars, blocking traffic, and threatening citizens trying to go to work (a pastime the Antifa protesters do not share).

When CNN's Jake Tapper described the Antifa attack as "violence," he was swiftly "corrected" by the blue-check brigade.[6] Defenders of Antifa blamed the violence on a "volatile" climate. One rioter, a former college philosophy professor named Eric Clanton, received three years' probation after beating someone about the head with a bike lock.[7] Chris Cuomo, while deploring the violence, nevertheless defended Antifa on CNN, praising its cause and insisting that "all punches are not equal morally.... [P]eople who show up to fight bigots are not to be judged the same as bigots."[8]

The left tries to romanticize the violence with which it accomplishes its goals, but its record is undeniably ugly. The book *Days of Rage* chronicles the violent left of the 1970s, when there were more than 2,500 domestic bombings in a single year. The airbrushed images of Bill Ayers, Bernardine Dohrn, Students for a Democratic Society, and the Weather

Underground, self-styled "revolutionaries" who espoused hate and violence, do not hold up under scrutiny. Fueled by rage and self-interest, they conducted arson and bomb attacks across the country, including at the U.S. Capitol and the Pentagon. These were supposedly humane bombings because they tried to let the targeted people escape, but they killed three of their own in an accidental explosion. During a domestic terrorist "war council" speech discussing the aesthetic of their fight, Dohrn invoked the Manson family: "We're about being crazy motherf—s and scaring the sh— out of honky America! ... Dig it! First they killed those pigs. Then they ate dinner in the same room with them. Then they even shoved a fork into the victim's stomach! Wild!"[9]

Wild, indeed. Neither Dohrn nor Ayers ever went to prison for their crimes.[10] Both went on to teach at respected universities and launch the presidential campaign of Barack Obama in their living room. The left never turned on or repudiated the '60s and '70s radicals, so it shouldn't be a surprise that it refuses to do the same with today's violent radicals.

Violence has increased in the era of Trump, having been sanctioned early on by some in media and Hollywood. Trump hadn't even taken office before the violent riots began. After the election in November 2016, ABC News caught leftists on video rioting in Portland, smashing windows of cars and businesses in protest.[11]

Hundreds were arrested in Inauguration Day riots,[12] which saw dumpsters set ablaze, businesses vandalized, and private property destroyed (one driver had his limo set on fire).[13] More than two hundred persons were arrested for the destruction.

In January 2017, a Trump supporter was taunted and knocked out by leftist protesters in Portland.[14] At the Women's March that month, the singer Madonna announced that she had "thought an awful lot about blowing up the White House."[15] The following month, the *Daily Mail* reported that there had been more than twelve thousand tweets since the inauguration demanding Trump's assassination.[16]

In March, the former attorney general Loretta Lynch sanctioned the riots, declaring, "It has been people, individuals who have banded together, ordinary people who simply saw what needed to be done and came together and supported those ideals who have made the difference. They've marched, they've bled, and yes, some of them died. This is hard. Every good thing is. We have done this before. We can do this again."[17]

Same month: violent masked rioters at Middlebury College attacked the libertarian scholar Charles Murray and Professor Allison Stanger, giving Stanger a concussion, and jumped on their vehicle as they tried to leave.[18]

In April rioters shut down numerous speeches at the University of California at Berkeley, even setting parts of their campus on fire. The madness continued that spring when the "comedian" Kathy Griffin posted a gruesome photo of herself holding a bloody decapitated Trump head, and the rapper Snoop Dogg released a video of himself acting out an assassination of the president. The actor Rob Reiner followed up with a call for an "all-out war" to "save Democracy."[19]

In June 2017 a sometime Bernie Sanders campaign volunteer with a history of leftist social media posts tried to assassinate Republican lawmakers during a practice for their annual congressional baseball game for charity. A hit list naming conservative members of the House Freedom Caucus was found in the assailant's van.[20] Afterward the HuffPost scrubbed its website of an op-ed declaring that impeachment of Trump "wasn't enough."[21]

There are hundreds of examples.

A high-ranking member of Moms Demand was charged with disorderly conduct after she screamed obscenities in the faces of two young girls for wearing pro-Trump t-shirts as they waited in a bakery to purchase cookies before church.[22]

In Indiana, someone shot at a truck with a "Make America Great Again" sticker;[23] the home of Ben Carson, the secretary of housing and urban development, was vandalized;[24] the high-profile Republicans Sarah Sanders and Ted Cruz were chased out of restaurants. In August 2017, far-left protesters and white supremacists clashed at a protest in Charlottesville, Virginia, over the removal of a Confederate statue, leaving one protester dead. Those on the left and right who came out to the rally were horrified.

As the number of such incidents mounted, Conservapedia.com began keeping a list of them. The left's response, however, was to announce a "surge" in *Trump*-inspired violence. Not so fast, replied David Harsanyi, who poked a thousand holes in a *"Washington Post* 'analysis' of domestic terrorism [that] argues that attacks from white supremacists and other 'far-right attackers' have been on the rise since Barack Obama's presidency and 'surged since President Trump took office.'" Noting that it is notoriously difficult to characterize and quantify such incidents, Harsanyi showed that the pretensions to scientific rigor in the reports of right-wing attacks and hate crimes were bogus.[25]

In 2017 Senator Rand Paul was assaulted by a neighbor so ferociously that he suffered five rib fractures and lost part of a lung. The assailant maintained that his anger stemmed from lawn care, not politics (he is a Democrat), but the attack was another case of a progressive expressing himself violently.[26]

Democratic Congressman Joaquin Castro made an excellent case for reforming campaign finance laws when he quasi-doxxed his own constituents in San Antonio who had donated to President Trump's campaign. The twin brother of Julian Castro, a former Obama cabinet secretary and candidate for president in 2020, Joaquin decided to make voters accountable to politicians by publishing the names and business affiliations of the offending San Antonians, tweeting, "Sad to see so many San Antonians as 2019 maximum donors to Donald Trump—the owner of @BillMillerBarBQ, owner of the @HistoricPearl, realtor Phyllis Browning, etc. Their contributions are fueling a campaign of hate that labels Hispanic immigrants as 'invaders.'" Castro attached a graphic to his tweet identifying forty-four donors, many of them retirees, by name.

The House GOP leader, Kevin McCarthy, blasted Castro, tweeting, "Targeting and harassing Americans because of their political beliefs is shameful and dangerous. What happened to 'when they go low, we go high?' Or does that no longer matter when your brother is polling at 1%? Americans deserve better."[27]

An unrepentant Castro noted that the information about donors came from public sources and repeated his charge "that President Trump spends donor money on thousands of ads about Hispanics 'invading' America."

Castro knew exactly what publicizing the names and businesses of Trump donors would accomplish. It was a threat, an act of intimidation. At least one of the persons on his list received death threats.[28] The unspoken message was that if you contribute to Trump, you might become a target of leftist harassment or worse.

To be fair, Castro's stunt received heavy criticism from both the right and left, giving me some hope that not all decency is gone from public discourse.[29]

This isn't different from the backlash felt by Stephen Ross, the chairman of the company that owns both SoulCycle and Equinox, who was shamed for privately hosting a fundraiser for Trump.[30] The left cannot separate the person from the issue. The person, therefore, should be afforded no privacy if he commits the sin of dissent.

When we left increasingly blue St. Louis, Missouri, for Texas in December 2013, I felt confident about the town to which we were moving. I'm a planner and a compulsive researcher, so I spent a few months examining a list of places in Texas where we might live. I knew what kind of church we would attend and that I had to be close to an airport, and we narrowed our choices down to three amazing towns. In one weekend we looked at twenty-one houses, which I rated and kept track of on a spreadsheet. We had twenty-four hours to have a first and final offer accepted before boarding our flight back to St. Louis to pack and move. We had just weeks to vacate our home, relocate my radio studio, *and* start my new second job at The Blaze in Irving, Texas. At some point, we thought, we would build a forever home, a place our parents might one day move into as well, a place where we would gather with our children as they grew and had kids of their own. We would take our time and not rush. I was thrilled with the town to which we moved. It was in a conservative, family-centered area where Sunday morning church traffic rivals that of Monday-through-Friday rush hour; a place where people are active and serve their community; a place where roots run deep.

Roots are important to me, but my and my children's relationship with many in my own family, most of whom are progressives, changed after I became a prominent conservative. It felt like the excommunication began gradually, growing more rigorous when I began appearing on Fox and CNN. A few of my relatives remained in touch, but otherwise my limb of the family tree was sawed off.

I had already endured abandonment by my father, and this was very much the same feeling. The hurt I felt was the realization that I knew *who* they were and *what* they believed, and I loved them anyway because they were *family*, my people first. I would have taken their side in a dispute on that principle alone, such is my Eddard Starkian loyalty. The people who listen to my program in southern Missouri, who send kindly words of encouragement or even disagreement, have grown to be more of a family to me than those who chose political allegiance over blood. I think this is when I finally began to see the great metamorphosis occurring in our country at every level, even in the fabric of the family.

We settled in Texas in a house on a cul-de-sac by a ranch. We joined the church we always wanted to attend, our kids settled into school, and I felt both lucky and grateful to have found such a piece of heaven on earth. Our welcoming neighbors had hearts for God and looked out for each other, and we grew to appreciate their fellowship.

While I genuinely loved and appreciated my neighbors in St. Louis, some listeners who disagreed would often make it known at my door or in the parking lot of my radio station, necessitating a security escort when disagreement was particularly high. I didn't feel free anymore, and when the opportunity to change the situation presented itself, I took it.

Life in our new home was idyllic. Because of my tumultuous childhood, however, I never have more anxiety than when things are *perfect*, because *perfect* doesn't last. I can handle crises, stress, negativity—I grew up in a storm of them. I'm always alert for the next storm so as to be in the best position to weather it. Sure enough, my perfect peace in Texas didn't last. Soon a far-left attorney in my community began making a stink about having to live in the same city with me. Later, as the noise of the 2016 election ascended to a shriek, people who disagree with me posted our address and photos of our home and published our phone number. I began receiving calls from people who threatened to murder me in my yard in front of my children. My kids couldn't ride their bikes up and down the street anymore. The neighbors kept a wary eye on the road and would text Chris if they saw a car they didn't recognize. So instead of taking our time and building a home as we had planned, we moved abruptly for safety's sake.

We took pains to conceal our new location and waited nearly five months before placing our home on the market. One evening, a month after we moved (but had not yet listed our old home), a neighbor frantically called Chris, telling him that a man was outside of our home, banging on our doors and windows. The neighbor's wife was terrified and called the police. The man had flown across the country to confront me after a San Francisco–based reporter vengefully posted photos of our new house after the Parkland massacre. That previously-mentioned attorney in my town ratcheted up the rhetoric by falsely charging that I had brandished a weapon at Beto O'Rourke supporters while voting in the 2018 midterm election and that the city was "looking into it." (Several city council members and the mayor of my town denounced the attorney's behavior on Facebook.)

Some of those who were infuriated by my support of the Second Amendment even threatened to shoot my dogs. Hate doesn't rely on reason. It thrives in its absence. Turning the object of a person's antipathy into something inhuman—a political issue, for instance—enables the hater to become more rabid, more partisan. Socialists and progressives have developed this kind of hate into an art form, treating people who hold certain *ideas* as though they were committing violent *acts*. Consider the MAGA hat phenomenon.

In April 2019 Atsu Mable, an immigrant from Togo who had become an American citizen in 2013, finished a hearty dinner and decided to enjoy the mild spring temperatures with a walk around his Maryland neighborhood, putting on a red "Make America Great Again" hat as he went out the door. Soon he was approached by two men who began to ridicule him for his hat. Mable told them he was entitled to his own views and attempted to walk away. According to the Montgomery County police, that's when the men began to pummel him, knocking him down onto the pavement.

Mable, who registered as a Republican during the 2016 presidential Trump candidacy, told the media that he wishes people would demonstrate tolerance. "They felt like a black man should not be wearing a Trump hat because it's like when you are black, you have to be a Democrat. I'll wear it again."[31]

In March 2019 Terry Price told his wife and kids to stop wearing MAGA hats after a disapproving leftist held a gun to his head at a Sam's Club. Fifty-seven-year-old James Phillips pointed a Glock in Price's face and said, "This is a good day for you to die." Phillips was arrested and charged with wanton endangerment. Price and his wife changed their party affiliation from Democrat to Republican, citing the increase in hate within their former party.[32]

That same month a school bus aide ripped fourteen-year-old Gunnar Johansson's MAGA hat off his head. Students were allowed to wear whatever hat they wanted to school in exchange for a March of Dimes donation. Closed-circuit TV captured the unnamed aide threatening the boy, "If you don't take that hat off . . . ."[33]

A month earlier, nineteen-year-old Ryan Salvagno confronted an eighty-one-year-old man wearing a MAGA hat outside a store in New Jersey.[34] The elderly man tried to get away with his groceries, but Salvagno grabbed the hat, threw the elderly man to the ground, and turned over his cart of groceries. He was charged with assault and harassment.

That same month eighteen-year-old Kenneth Jones knocked a MAGA hat off the head of a seventeen-year-old classmate, shouting "Are you proud of what you are wearing?" Jones grabbed the hat and the pro-Trump banner the victim carried. He was charged with assault and harassment.

Also in February 2019, Bryton Turner was dining in a Massachusetts restaurant when Rosiane Santos, a Brazilian national illegally in the United States, tried to shove Turner's face into his food, knocked his MAGA hat from his head, and screamed invectives at him. Charged with assault and disorderly conduct, Santos was taken into custody by ICE, which released her but initiated deportation proceedings.[35]

Jonathan Sparks, wearing a MAGA hat and carrying a sign reading "Vote Jobs not Mobs—Vote Republican," was attacked in March 2019 in Tucson by Daniel Zaroes Brito. A legislative assistant to Congressman Raul Grijalva, Brito screamed "Nazi," "Hitler," and "Trump" during the assault, which sent Sparks to the hospital.[36]

In Overland Park, Kansas, an employee of a clothing store was fired after saying "f—you" to a fourteen-year-old customer for wearing a MAGA hat. Video of the exchange went viral, prompting the store to fire the employee.[37]

In July 2018 thirty-year-old Kino Jimenez assaulted sixteen-year-old Hunter Richard and his friends, unprovoked, in a hamburger restaurant, because Richard was wearing a red MAGA hat. Jimenez was captured on camera cursing the teens before throwing soda in Richard's face and ripping the hat off Richard's head—and some of Richard's hair with it. Arrested and charged with theft, Jimenez reportedly lost his job.[38]

On Mother's Day 2018 some Cheesecake Factory employees in Miami reportedly taunted and threatened a young man as he dined with his girlfriend and her family. Witnesses said the harassment continued as the family left the restaurant. The manager followed the customers out and told them the employees would be dealt with, and Cheesecake

Factory responded: "No guest should ever feel unwelcomed in one of our restaurants and we are taking this matter very seriously. Upon learning of this incident, we immediately apologized to the guests in person. We are conducting an investigation and will take the appropriate corrective action."[39]

The most infamous case of MAGA hat rage began on the steps of the Lincoln Memorial in January 2019 and nearly ruined the lives of a group of teenage boys from Covington Catholic High School in Kentucky. The students had just participated in the annual March for Life and were waiting at their appointed rendezvous point when a group of wackos calling themselves the Black Hebrew Israelites began shouting racial and sexual slurs at the boys. An elderly American Indian and professional activist named Nathan Phillips then approached one of the boys, Nick Sandmann, and began beating a drum in his face. Sandmann stood politely, awkwardly smiling in an attempt to deescalate the situation. "Where were the adults?" you may ask. They were taunting the children.

But Sandmann and some of the other teens were wearing MAGA hats, newly-purchased souvenirs of their trip—all the evidence anyone on the left needed that the kids were racists. The perpetually distressed damsel Alyssa Milano declared, "The red MAGA hat is the new white hood," charging that the boys were "flaunting their entitlement and displaying toxic masculinity."[40] When called out on her rhetoric she doubled down, stating that the MAGA hat was a symbol of "white nationalism and racism." "So, I won't apologize to these boys," she added, "Or anyone who wears that hat. But I will thank them. I will thank them for lighting a fire underneath the conversation about systemic racism and misogyny in this country and the role President Donald Trump has had in cultivating it and making it acceptable."[41]

The media pushed the "MAGA = racism" theme:

- Vox, January 23, 2019: "The hats extinguished pretty much any benefit of the doubt a liberal observer might have given these kids."[42]

- CNN, March 12, 2019: "Why Trump's MAGA hats have become a potent symbol of racism."[43]

As much as I loathed the Pepto-pink pussy-cat hats worn by the über-feminists who flooded the streets of the capital, assaulting one of these women never crossed my mind. Probably because I'm an adult and grew up in the late 1980s and early '90s when women wore lace cuffs under tight-rolled jeans, so I've seen worse. (I also felt a twinge of pity for them. If that's what they thought the female copulatory organ resembled, they may need to see a medical professional.)

Former *Think Progress* flunky Zack Ford virtue-flexed hard with an entire column on how he unfriended a woman over a clothing accessory: "Specifically, I share a story in today's newsletter about my decision to unfriend someone I've known since high school over her decision to wear a MAGA hat. I gave her a choice, and she chose the hat over me."[44]

To be fair, I would drop any dude that devolved into a toddler and demanded that I not wear a specific hat so his feelings wouldn't be hurt. In fact, out of spite, I'd probably buy several more of the same hat and wear them all at once, ridiculously, every time I was around him because absurdity needs a companion.

The red hat fervor hit peak woke when the actor Jussie Smollett, of *Empire* fame, tried to capitalize on it with his hate-crime hoax. Smollett reportedly hired two brothers from Nigeria to pose as Trump fans and walk around Chicago late at night in a blizzard, confront Smollett, and ask him if he was that "F-word N-word." Dave Chappelle's commentary on this prank from his *Sticks & Stones* Netflix special is hysterical:

> Everybody was furious, especially in Hollywood.... "Justice for Juicy" and all this sh**.... For some reason, African Americans, we were like oddly quiet.... What they didn't understand is that we were supporting him with our silence. Because we understood that this n—— was clearly lying. None of these details added up at all.... "Hey man, aren't you

that f—— n—— from *Empire?*" What the f—? Does that
sound like how white people talk? ... It sounds like something
that I would say! ... If you a racist and homophobic you don't
even know who this n—— is! You don't watch Empire....

He said they put a rope around his neck. Has anyone here
ever been to Chicago? All right, so you been there. Now tell
me, how much rope do you remember seeing? ... Like when
did you get mugged, n——, 1850? Who's got rope?[45]

After Smollett, the red hat rage began to turn.

On the Fourth of July, 2019, in Washington, D.C., an anti-Trump
bro congratulated himself for making scene in a restaurant by berating
a tourist in a MAGA hat, tweeting:

Just got thrown out of Hill Country DC for standing up to a
Nazi. Don't go there ever again. They support Trump and
Nazis. @HillCountryWDC @HillCountryBBQ

Guy wears MAGA hat at my favorite restaurant. I say
"hey are you from dc?" He says "no." I say "we don't tolerate
racism in this city." His girlfriend then physically jabs fingers
into my chest and starts threatening me. Management tells
me to leave, not woman who assaulted me.[46]

Somewhat surprisingly, the public was not very sympathetic. A D. C.
denizen had the best response to the hat-stunt in his own series of
tweets:

Every day I see hundreds of tourists walking through my
area.... A few days ago, I sat down to grab a quick bite before
heading to a housewarming party. There was an extremely
kind family of four sitting near me. They were extremely nice
to me when I asked them to hand me something down the
counter. Two boys and their parents. When they left the

restaurant, they all put back on their MAGA hats and began walking towards the White House, and for some reason, I began to worry about them.... I had a lump in my throat as I feared that someone might say something. I then quickly brushed it away. Now that this Hill Country incident has happened, I would like to make one thing clear to my fellow D. C. residents. Yes, we live here. No none of us agree on everything, but this isn't our city. This city belongs to everyone in the United States.... So yes, you may disagree with our visitors, but they have just as much of a right to be here as you. So treat them with the same respect that you know that they would treat you.... They shouldn't have to fear being here due to politics. And I am ashamed of my fellow city-dwellers.[47]

That response gave me a weird feeling of hope that perhaps we are not too terribly far gone yet, that there are remnants of old-fashioned respect and tolerance out there. Division grifters are on the prowl, however, eager to destroy what common ground we have left.

The right targets ideology. The left targets people. To the left, the issues are indistinguishable from people. They cannot separate the soul from the stance. It's why the left prevents its own members from finding common ground with anyone on the right, as it did when Karamo Brown said something nice about Sean Spicer. Human sympathy tears away the veil and shows the person as a person, something more than an issue. Progressivism loses influence when people find common ground. Even more dangerous than Brown and Spicer's coming together was their coming together on a prime-time TV show. It was an opportunity to mainstream common ground, and the left revolted.

Television and film are the left's territory, the stage from which it pushes its ideology. Calling Spicer a "sweet guy" not only humanizes Spicer but makes it harder to hate him when you get to know him, when you see him in a setting outside of the political sphere he represents. Intentionally or not, Brown vouched for Spicer. That's how the left looks at it, and subconsciously that's how viewers, millions of average Americans across the country, interpret it.

If a celebrity says he likes something or says someone is cool, he influences others. People who admire him will adopt that opinion. Brown said Spicer was a good guy, and Brown has a lot of fans who might also think Spicer is a good guy. Brown was out of line, so he came in for a good old-fashioned shaming from the rage mob. They accused him of betraying his convictions by daring to recognize any good qualities in someone who votes differently. Others bizarrely inferred that Brown, a black man, somehow supported the "racism" of the administration. Eventually he worried about his family's safety, just as the mob hoped. Most people crumble under those circumstances. But Brown—whose politics are probably lightyears from my own, earned my respect when he refused to back down. A simple Instagram post might not seem consequential, but it was a powerful gesture. His refusal to denounce Spicer to the rage mob gave me hope that others might see his stand and do the same.

Joe Biden proved to lack the strength Brown exhibited. In the spring of 2019, while Biden was campaigning in Nebraska, he called Vice President Mike Pence a "decent guy." Not a "good guy," or even a "wonderful guy," just decent. A shoulder shrug.

The reaction from the rage mob came swiftly. Cynthia Nixon, who was running for governor of New York, tweeted: "@JoeBiden you've just called America's most anti-LGBT elected leader a 'decent guy.' Please consider how this falls on the ears of our community." Blandly accepting the slur that Pence is indecently anti-gay, Biden tweeted in response: "You're right, Cynthia. I was making a point in a foreign policy context, that under normal circumstances a vice president wouldn't be given a silent reaction on the world stage. But there is nothing decent about being anti-LGBTQ rights, and that includes the vice president."

Pence's actual views were irrelevant to progressives. He is a Republican. Calling him "decent" is the same grievous sin as calling Spicer a "sweet guy." But Biden bent a knee to the rage mob. Weeks later, he remarked (without blushing), "I get criticized for saying anything nice about a Republican. Folks, that's not who we are. We don't treat the opposition as the enemy. We might even say a nice word every once in a while about a Republican when they do something good."[48]

In his day, Biden was as partisan and divisive as any of contemporaries. He seems mellow now only because his party has moved past him. He's a relic from Democrats' bygone days. In the ascendency are those who embrace division, preferring a hateful accusation to a reasoned retort. Biden isn't innocent in all of this; his own brand of partisan rancor set the stage. You can hear the surrender in his voice when he implores his fellow Democrats to not see as enemies their fellow citizens across the aisle. He knows that time has passed, and his responses on the campaign trail suggest that he realizes that he, a party patriarch, bears some responsibility for reigning in the very people that he used as attack dogs for so long. He sanctioned the extremists because the extremists drove voters. Though he probably abhorred the violence, he ignored it because the violence brought chilled dissent. That was the goal. Nancy Pelosi hasn't condemned the attacks on MAGA hat–wearing Americans, but she has referred to the slogan as "Make America White Again."[49]

The language sanctions the violence. If you convince people that a clothing accessory is a symbol of racism, akin to the white hood of the Klan, then yes, you are likely to excite people who have no qualms about attacking the "racists" who wear it.

Progressives pretend to be martyrs, engaging in fascistic behavior to crush what they call fascism. The violence of Antifa is justified because the cause is just. They are the militant, violent left, sanctioned by the politicians who refuse to condemn their violence, defended by talking heads on cable news, supported to make decent people think twice before wearing a red hat or sharing an opinion. The commentator Peggy Noonan has ruefully noted that Americans have grown rude, particularly in discourse, ignoring the admonitions of the Founders about the virtue and grace necessary to keep the republic they gave us.[50]

CHAPTER FIVE

Milkshake Ducks and Rage Mobs

*"The whole Internet loves Milkshake Duck, a lovely duck that drinks milkshakes! *5 seconds later* We regret to inform you the duck is racist."*

—*@pixelatedboat*

The term "milkshake duck," which Ben Ward (known on Twitter as @pixelatedboat) coined, refers to someone or something that is adorable, innocent, unobjectionable, and therefore unifying—until someone reveals something embarrassing or condemnable in his background or finds something objectionable in his social media footprint from years past.

Twenty-one-year-old Kyler Murray worked hard his entire life to get to where he was—the recipient of the 2018 Heisman Trophy. What should have been one of the happiest moments of Murray's life was ruined by a twit named Scott Gleeson, whose day job consists of trolling athletes' Twitter archives back to their teenage years to see if they ever typed anything untoward. While Murray isn't your average football player, he was your average fourteen-year-old, ribbing his friends with remarks like "y'all are queers." Sensing his big byline break, Gleeson suggested that these tweets revealed that Murray hates gay people and thus must be ineligible to win the Heisman. What's worse, Gleeson thought that they were newsworthy. Good job, man! You nearly took out a twenty-one-year-old and ruined his life forever.

In any normal culture, an adult man's obsessing over a teenager's tweets would raise eyebrows and draw concerned looks. But our culture believes *some* people should be held responsible for the indiscretions of youth. It depends on who you are and whom you have offended. If you're Beto O'Rourke, the son of a judge, who in his mid-twenties drove drunk down the interstate, crashed into another vehicle, and attempted to flee the scene, your impeccably progressive political views wipe the slate clean when you're ready to run for office. But if you're just a football player who has accidentally sinned against the gay lobby, it's not so easy. But Murray stepped up. Even though it was obvious that he'd been ripping on his friends facetiously seven years earlier, he dutifully issued an apology the next morning to quell the rage mob: "I used a poor choice of word that doesn't reflect who I am or what I believe. I did not intend to single out any individual or group."

It's disturbing that Murray had to explain to a bunch of shrieking adults that teenagers sometimes say stupid and careless things. The swiftness of his response gave him the upper hand. Lowering their pitchforks and torches, the dejected rage mob retreated. They weren't really concerned about Murray's heart and mind. They just wanted to show off their power.

Something similar happened to twenty-four-year-old Carson King, an Iowa State football fan who became an overnight legend when he was pictured on ESPN's *College GameDay* holding a sign that read, "Busch Light Supply Needs Replenished [sic]. Venmo Carson-King-25." In moments he had a thousand dollars in his account. As the thousand dollars turned into several thousands, King decided to donate the money to a children's hospital in Iowa City. King informed the public of the plan on social media, and the donations took off.

Anheuser-Busch responded by matching the donations. They also told King, "We'll throw in some of that Busch Light you were looking for."

And then he was Milkshake Ducked.

After running an article headlined "Meet Carson King, the 'Iowa Legend' who's raised more than $1 million for charity off of a sign asking for beer money," the *Des Moines Register* followed with a tweet: "On Monday evening, *Register* reporter Aaron Calvin was assigned to interview King for a profile.[1] On Tuesday, as he worked to write the story, he did a routine background check on King that included a review of publicly visible social media posts, a standard part of a reporter's work on a profile. Calvin found two racist jokes that King had posted on Twitter in 2012. Calvin asked King about them and he expressed deep regret."[2]

As a matter of fact, scouring the tweets of a sixteen-year-old who would later raise a million dollars for a children's hospital is not "a standard part of a reporter's work." It's hackery. It had nothing to do with the story. Is the new "standard" to include what everyone wrote about when he was sixteen years old?

King got in front of the damage, holding a press conference in which he apologized for his dumb, teenaged behavior:

> I am so embarrassed and stunned to reflect on what I thought was funny when I was sixteen years old. I want to sincerely apologize.
>
> Thankfully, high school kids grow up and hopefully become responsible and caring adults. I think my feelings are better summed up by a post from just three years ago:
>
> "Until we as a people learn that racism and hate are learned behaviors, we won't get rid of it. Tolerance towards others is the first step." —July 8, 2016
>
> I am sharing this information tonight because I feel a responsibility to all of the people who have donated money.
>
> I cannot go back and change what I posted when I was a sixteen-year-old. I can apologize and work to improve every day and make a meaningful difference in people's lives.

And, I am so very thankful for the generosity of the thousands of people who have donated to our fundraising push
for the Stead Family Children's Hospital.[3]

As genuine and heartfelt as King's remarks were, the damage was
already done. Anheuser-Busch announced that it was severing all ties
with him and would not match any new funds for the children's hospital. The *Register* went on pretending it hadn't attempted to wreck his
life. A final twist in the story, however, brought some poetic justice
when Aaron Calvin's old tweets were unearthed. The reporter who
provoked the shaming of Carter King, it was revealed, himself had a
seven-year-long record (as an adult) of racist, misogynist, and homophobic statements. As the rage mob descended on Calvin, I shed no
tears for the media hacks who turn their bylines into cudgels, bringing
the cancel culture down on the head of a guy who said hurtful things
as a teenager but demonstrated more growth than the reporter who
shamed him. When does it end?

The rage mob is the modern-day Spanish Inquisition. Comprising
social justice warriors and those who seek attention for hurt feelings,
it moves from tantrum to tantrum like a swarm of locusts, overwhelming its targets, ruining their lives, leaving anguish in its wake, and
further dividing America. Companies are terrified of it, which is why
most will promptly drop associations with anyone determined to be
problematic by the rage mob. The tactics of the rage mob aren't particularly sophisticated—they require numbers, and their weapon of
choice is shame.

It's odd, though, to shame people for a lack of morals when contem-
porary culture is defined by its attack on virtue. The rage mob gives the
impression that it seeks an apology, but really it seeks a reckoning. It is
interested not in persuasion or in righting the wrongs of the heart, not
in healing or reconciliation, but in destruction. So commonplace is the
mob's behavior that their targets have naturally fallen into a couple of
different categories.

The Milkshake Duck and Problematic Fave

Kyler Murray technically isn't a milkshake duck. He was already well known, whereas a true milkshake duck is someone who instantaneously emerges from obscurity and then just as quickly becomes the object of opprobrium.

Now don't mistake me—sometimes people do things that deserve universal condemnation. Sometime they deserve a milkshake ducking. We are the worst and best enforcers of social behavior, and there are times we have to hold the line for decency's sake, for humanity's sake—but without losing our decency and humanity. The problem is that the usual enforcers do not always abide by the standards they set for others.

Some classic milkshake ducks:

Target: Candace Payne
Crime: White privilege

In May 2016, Payne, a mom in Texas, visited her local Kohl's and bought herself a Chewbacca mask—not just any Chewbacca mask, but one that makes the sound of Chewbacca's bear-yell.[4] She live-streamed herself on Facebook wearing a Star Wars t-shirt while unboxing the mask in her car. Her joy was uncontainable, contagious, and unrehearsed.

"That's not me making that noise!" she yelled. "That's the mask!!" before erupting into uncontrollable laughter. "I'm such a happy Chewbacca! ... It's the simple joys!" With all the nastiness in the world, it was a palate-cleanser for the soul to watch someone derive so much joy from wearing a mask. I laughed because she was laughing, and her laugh sounds like one of those perfectly engineered movie laughs, as if Paramount audio engineers confected the perfect belly laugh. The video, a bit more than three minutes long, was both hysterical and magical in that it reminded me how when I was a kid, the simplest things—like new markers, a coloring book, and a snack pack of pudding while watching the Muppets—made my day. Apparently others thought so too. Her video is the most-watched Facebook video of all time, with 140 million views. Delighted with the free advertising, Kohl's bestowed $2,500 in in gift cards and Star Wars toys on Payne. Appearances on network morning shows were followed by more gifts and scholarships for her children.

But milkshake duck.

The Internet began to turn on the mom who, for nearly four minutes, had brought so much joy to so many. First came a TMZ report that Chewbacca Mom was charging twenty dollars for autographs at the Dallas Fan Expo, where her booth was right next to Jack Gleeson's (Joffrey from *Game of Thrones*). Some thought she was starting to get greedy, although why would anyone go to a fan expo and complain about someone who found fame on the Internet appearing at the expo as an Internet celebrity? Yes, Internet celebrity is a thing now, and if Billy Dee Williams's son can appear at a Comic Con under the banner "Billy Dee Williams's son," and if YouTube personalities with fewer lifetime views than Payne got for one Facebook video can commandeer the airwaves, then why shouldn't the lady with one of the most-watched videos ever have a table and charge for autographs? (For the record, it's less than what Alice Cooper charges, and I know because I was in line for him and have his signed picture on my office wall.)

Joy often turns into jealousy, as it did with Chewbacca Mom. People began to question why she was getting scholarships for herself and her kids, money, and trips. Perhaps it wasn't because of her video, some speculated, but because she was white.[5] Others complained about her Christian beliefs, charging that she went over the top when she broadcast herself singing to a piano version of Michael Jackson's "Heal the World" after the ambush and murder of five police officers in downtown Dallas.[6]

The most damaging charge, though, was that her good fortune was the result of her "white privilege." The Internet wondered why a black girl named Kayla Newman, known online as Peaches Monroee, didn't profit comparably for coining the phrase "on fleek," which numerous companies incorporated into their merchandising. Newman, however, hasn't gone unnoticed. The *New York Times* profiled her, detailing her dreams of running a beauty empire,[7] as did *Teen Vogue*.[8] She should be paid by the retailers that use her phrase, but why pit her against Payne? You don't lift people up by tearing someone else down—can we be happy that the older woman found opportunity with a Chewbacca mask and celebrate the potential of the younger woman, who with the help of media attention and her catch phrase, has a promising future? Payne caught lightning in a bottle with her short video. I sometimes think people become bored with being happy, especially in this culture where they crave conflict.

Target: Ken Bone
Crime: Not being Mr. Rogers

Ken Bone is considered to be the first real milkshake duck. He attracted attention at the second 2016 presidential debate, where he was one of the audience members selected to ask a question of the candidates. America was introduced to a rotund, bespectacled man in a festive red sweater identified at the bottom of the screen as "Kenneth Bone, uncommitted voter." Posing a straightforward and sensible question about energy policy, he came off as the most wholesome person in politics at that moment. Television footage at the end of the debate captured him wandering around the stage, preserving the historic moment not with an iPhone but with a quaint disposable camera. Within the hour, several major media organizations had published stories about him, and there was a national run on red sweaters. Explaining his choice of apparel, Bone said: "I had a really nice olive suit that I love a great deal and that my mother would have been very proud to see me wearing on television, but apparently I've gained about thirty pounds, and when I went to get in my car the morning of the debate, I split the seat of my pants all the way open. So, the red sweater is plan B, and I'm glad it works out."[9]

Bone appeared on *Jimmy Kimmel Live*, the *Daily Show* featured him, and the Halloween costumer Yandy's "Ken Bone" costume sold out in just a day. Then Bone participated in a Reddit AMA ("Ask Me Anything") using his Reddit name StanGibson18, annnnnnnnd … Bone was milkshake ducked.

Digging into his comment history, Redditors found all sorts of material that belied Bone's wholesome image.

Bone is luckier than other milkshake ducks. He didn't have to disappear into the shadows to escape the rage mob. Today he hosts a podcast and is still on social media, discussing all manner of topics, including politics.

Target: Carter Wilkerson, the Wendy's Chicken Nuggets kid
Crime: Tweeting to a no-no account

Wilkerson, a sixteen-year-old who loves Wendy's chicken nuggets, asked the fast-food purveyor over Twitter how many retweets it would take for him to get a year's worth of free chicken nuggets.

"18 million" was Wendy's verified reply.

At first, Wilkerson was crestfallen, but he went on to break Ellen DeGeneres's Oscar selfie record by getting a total of 3.5 million retweets after begging Twitter "help me. a man needs his nuggs." Every now and then people on the Internet like to take a break from biting each other's throats out and reconcile over something entirely silly, such as this. Wilkerson brought the Internet together, attracting help from everyone from "Nature Boy" Ric Flair to NASCAR driver Michael McDowell, who affixed a #NuggsForCarter decal on his car's bumper.[10]

Wait for it…

Then came the milkshake ducking.

The Internet discovered that Wilkerson had once tweeted (along with other account names) to the @Menininist account (now suspended, of course), a parody account that Al Bundy would have operated were he a real person.

Wilkerson still got his nuggs.

Target: Nancy Rommelmann and Ristretto Roasters
Crime: Criticizing #MeToo

A small chain of Oregon coffee shops, popular with the locals and an employer of hipsters, was milkshake ducked. Camila Coddou, an ex-employee of Ristretto Roasters, came across Nancy Rommelmann's "#MeNeither" YouTube videos, in which Rommelmann questioned certain aspects of the #MeToo movement. Whereas normal people would hear something with which they disagree and simply not watch (it's a *YouTube video* for crying out loud; you *don't have to click it*), Coddou decided she would accuse Rommelmann of being dangerous with all her opinions and emailed the letter to a bunch of newspapers and to the employees of Ristretto Roasters, including its owner, Din Johnson—Rommelmann's husband—accusing Rommelmann of posing a threat to assault survivors with her dangerous opinions, thereby creating an unsafe space at the cafe for female employees. The local media, because they're outright loons, wouldn't let the story go. Meanwhile thirty current and former Ristretto employees declared in an open letter, "We believe it is a business owner's responsibility to create a safe and supportive working environment for their employees. Invalidating assault survivors throws into question the safety of Ristretto Roasters as a workplace and has the potential to create a demoralizing and hostile environment for employees and customers alike. This cannot be tolerated."[11]

I'm sure Coddou is concerned for customers. But does anyone seriously believe that she's going to be assaulted in Nancy's husband's coffee shop because the boss's wife questions a movement that was co-opted by people with a political agenda?

Despite Johnson's pleading that Rommelmann doesn't own the business, the rage mob didn't care. Her opinions were bad. The business is on shaky ground as of this writing. Wholesale accounts were closed, the rage mob bombarded its social media accounts, and one of its shops has closed.

The insane thing is that Rommelmann is a progressive. Being boycotted by other progressives. The left eats its own.

Cancel Culture

Cancel culture is a tactic of the rage mob that works best on celebrities (even new Internet celebrities, as evidenced by milkshake duck). If a celebrity says or does something wrong, everything associated with him will be pressured to drop the association. The payoff for the rage mob is bigger than that for targeting random people on Twitter. It makes the mob look unbeatable, like a cultural god. I can't think of a better example of the mob's preference for destruction over redemption than the story of the comedian Kevin Hart.

Beginning back in 2009, Hart made a few jokes about LGBT people on Twitter. "Yo if my son comes home & try's 2 play with my daughters doll house," he tweeted, "I'm going 2 break it over his head & say n my voice 'stop that's gay.'"[12] He also tweeted that Damon Wayans's avatar looked like "a gay bill board for AIDS." He was also accused of making LGBT-insensitive jokes in a standup routine in 2010.

In December 2018 it was announced that Hart was to host the Oscars. He confirmed the news on Instagram: "I am blown away simply because this has been a goal on my list for a long time.... To be able to join the legendary list of hosts that have graced that stage is unbelievable." The SJW rage mob convened and chased Hart off the stage as host. He posted a video to Instagram explaining how the Academy asked him to apologize for his past tweets or step down from hosting the Oscars. He declined, stating in his video: "I passed on the apology.... I've addressed this several times. This is not the first time this has come up. I've addressed it. I've spoken on it. I've said where the rights and wrongs were."[13]

The rage mob's targets aren't supposed to refuse to surrender. Public resistance demonstrates the limitations of its power. The mob went harder at Hart, while his own fans debated whether the comedian owned an apology and how many times must one apologize before the apology quota is met. While the mob raged, Hart tweeted:

I have made the choice to step down from hosting this year's Oscar's ... because I do not want to be a distraction on a night that should be celebrated by so many amazing, talented artists. I sincerely apologize to the LGBTQ community for my insensitive words from my past.

I'm sorry that I hurt people. I am evolving and want to continue to do so. My goal is to bring people together not tear us apart. Much love & appreciation to the Academy. I hope we can meet again.[14]

Hart appeared on *Ellen*, explaining his choice to step down and addressing societal expectations of perfection:

Either my apology is accepted or it isn't. Either I can move forward or I can't. But you can't grow as a person without mistakes. You don't know what perfection is unless you've experienced imperfection. So I don't know [what] the perfect individual society is now looking for, but it's not me. I'll be the first to say it, it's not me. I'm an open book.[15]

Hart accurately explained that this wasn't an accident:

It was an attack, a malicious attack on my character. That's an attack to end me, that's not an attack to stop the Oscars, people don't understand, that's an attack to end me.... This was my first time in the fire. It was an attack to end all relationships.... It's bigger than just the Oscars, it's about the people out there now finding the success in damaging a celebrity.[16]

Yes, the mob doesn't care for dialogue or discussion; it will sacrifice the exchange of ideas on the altar of destruction. DeGeneres said she had called the Academy of Motion Picture Arts and Sciences, which told her that it still wanted Hart to host the awards ceremony. He declined, however, because the mob was going to make him pay for his decade-old tweets in perpetuity. Said DeGeneres: "There are so many haters out there, don't listen to them. There's a small group of people out there who are very, very loud. I want you to host the Oscars."

DeGeneres's handling of the interview was incredibly brave and a lesson in graciousness. I was astounded when the rage mob turned and began attacking her. She is one of the rarest types of entertainers—her first talent isn't humor. It's unity, common ground. You cannot pigeon-hole her fans. While she's been politically involved, she's never mean about it and has never once, that I've seen, shown disrespect to either political side. Again, it's why I say I was astounded and, frankly, angry when the rage mob turned from Hart and targeted her. They proved Hart's point entirely: they were not going to allow a Hart to redeem himself, and they tried to vilify DeGeneres for the crime of demonstrating forgiveness and publicizing redemption to the world.

CNN's Don Lemon scolded, "Apologizing and moving on does not make the world a better place for people who are gay or who are trans-gender. Being an ally does." For Lemon, it seems, apologies are meaning-less unless they are made in exactly the manner that the mob demands—nothing less.

The worst rage mob I've ever seen was the one that in 2015 descended on Justine Sacco, a previously unknown corporate communications person at the media company IAC. I watched it happen in real time on Twitter as the thirty-year-old Sacco was flying from New York to South Africa to visit family. From the *New York Times*:

> [Sacco] began tweeting acerbic little jokes about the indigni-
> ties of travel. There was one about a fellow passenger on the
> flight from John F. Kennedy International Airport: "'Weird
> German Dude: You're in First Class. It's 2014. Get some
> deodorant.' —Inner monologue as I inhale BO. Thank God
> for pharmaceuticals." Then, during her layover at Heathrow:
> "Chilly—cucumber sandwiches—bad teeth. Back in Lon-
> don!" And on Dec. 20, before the final leg of her trip to Cape

Town: "Going to Africa. Hope I don't get AIDS. Just kidding.
I'm white!"[17]

By the time she landed in Cape Town, eleven hours later, her AIDS
tweet, which she would later explain was mocking the Western idea that
AIDS was strictly an African concern, had gone viral. Sacco was about
to learn that sarcasm doesn't play well on Twitter, especially in an era
where nuance is dead, purposeful mischaracterization is fuel, and literal
meaning is king.

The hashtag #HasJustineLandedYet was the top worldwide trend.
The *Times* noted that the reaction to her tweet was in part a way for
people to pass the time. Someone even traveled to her destination in
South Africa to take a photo of her at the airport to show the world that
Justine had in fact landed. In the meantime, her co-workers had tweeted
their outrage, and her employer had publicly denounced her tweet. Someone remarked that people hadn't obsessed over a landing like this since
Apollo 11. Sacco's life was ruined. She cut short her vacation to see family
in South Africa; they were ashamed of her. Her public shaming cost her
her job, her friends, even her ability to date. (Googling a prospective
romantic interest is the first thing people do now.)

Sacco managed to turn her life around, but it isn't the same as before.
She did get an apology from one of the people who led the media charge
against her. After the rage mob had moved on to the next transgressor,
she asked Sam Biddle of Gawker's Valleywag tech publication to meet
her for dinner, to make the 2D target 3D.[18] It's harder to hate someone
when you meet him in real life, away from the anger that permeates
Twitter. Sacco realized the problem is easy access to a bullhorn and the
desire to be valued, even by invisible people one speaks with only through
an app. Normally one's dumbest moments would live in the shadows of
one's offline life, but people's eagerness to overshare everything gives
those momentary lapses into stupidity a worldwide audience.

Sometimes you don't need to say anything offensive at all; the offense
is wrongthink. The mob targets persons who seem in any way supportive

of Trump. Nick Vallelonga was targeted simply because he had liked and
responded to one of Trump's tweets.

Vallelonga, the Oscar-winning producer and writer of *Green Book*,
experienced the wrath of the rage mob when it transpired that in November
2015 he had expressed agreement with Trump's tweet "I watched when
the World Trade Center came tumbling down. And I watched in Jersey
City, New Jersey, where thousands and thousands of people were cheering
as that building was coming down. Thousands of people were cheering."[19]
Vallelonga replied "100% correct. Muslims in Jersey City cheering when
towers went down. I saw it, as you did, possibly on local CBS news."

Vallelonga groveled before the *Hollywood Reporter*: "I want to
apologize. I spent my life trying to bring this story of overcoming differ-
ences and finding common ground to the screen, and I am incredibly
sorry to everyone associated with *Green Book*." He added, "I especially
deeply apologize to the brilliant and kind Mahershala Ali, and all members of the Muslim faith, for the hurt I have caused. I am also sorry to
my late father who changed so much from Dr. Shirley's friendship, and
I promise this lesson is not lost on me. *Green Book* is a story about love,
acceptance and overcoming barriers, and I will do better."[20]

There was a slight problem, however. The *Washington Post* and
other outlets characterized Trump's tweet as an Islamophobic falsehood,
but as the Daily Wire noted, the *Washington Post* itself had reported
celebrations by Muslims in Jersey City within hours of the destruction
of the World Trade Center.[21] Trump may have exaggerated the number
of celebrants, but the *New York Times*, the *San Francisco Chronicle*,
and various New York radio stations had carried reports of such
celebrations.

So Vallelonga was quite possibly telling the truth about his own
experience but forced to deny it because it conflicted with other politically correct narratives.

Even knitters are getting woke.

Karen Templer, a knitter and purveyor of yarn, posted on her blog
in early 2019 that she was going to India as part of her year of wearing

more color.[22] Every wokescold with an Internet connection shamed her, trolled her, bullied her until she prostrated herself before her accusers. A typical comment:

> Karen, I'd ask you to re-read what you wrote and think about how your words feed into a colonial/imperialist mindset toward India and other non-Western countries. Multiple times you compare the idea of going to India to the idea of going to another planet—how do you think a person from India would feel to hear that?

If someone from India, excited about coming to the United States for the first time, wrote that it was like going to Mars, would anyone be upset? And yet the responses to Templer's post were beyond parody:

> I have read through the entire post again, and I am ashamed to say that I failed to consider the impact of this post on all of us non-white people. I skipped over the offensive parts because this space is so important to my well being. But my heart hurts, and I won't be able to live with myself unless I acknowledge the pain to me and others like me of the words used. I am no longer going to say nothing.[23]

This person's "heart hurts" because some chick got excited about visiting India and wearing colorful clothes? This absurd reaction is an effect of *too much Internet*. The solution: *Get off the Internet*. Vox, the Internet equivalent of the person at a party who, after too much chardonnay, turns into an expert on everything, ran a story headlined "The Knitting Community Is Reckoning with Racism."[24] I don't know which is more ridiculous—calling Templer's celebration of the beauty of another culture "racist" or referring to the "knitting community."

Just to reiterate: wokescold law says it's racist to celebrate the beauty of other cultures.

I supposed the wokescold mob would have preferred that Templer look down her nose at India's poverty, inequality, and discriminatory caste system. But no, this knitter simply wanted to celebrate the good about the country, and the reward for her goodwill was the rage mob.

Other knitters who deplored the sheer insanity of the level-burgundy wokescold alarm consuming Instagram knitters were themselves trolled to the point of closing or privatizing their Instagram accounts. Maria Tusken remarked:

> There was a very intense social justice issue that started infil-trating Instagram a few weeks ago. I would say it was very hostile, and people were being attacked and threatened and accused of things—small businesses, like mine, or slightly bigger with a few employees but still very small—all in the name of this social justice issue. And everyone was saying, "It's a conversation." But it is not a conversation. It's a one-sided … belief? And there was no room for discussion. It was just arguments; trolling; bullying.[25]

An eighteen-year-old from Utah named Keziah Daum found what she called a "beautiful, modest" dress to wear to her prom at Woods Cross High School. She was proud of the beautiful gown and posted her prom photos on social media. An older college male named Jeremy Lam felt that he needed to publicly berate a girl he didn't know over her prom dress, so he promptly retweeted her photos and wrote, "My culture is NOT your g*ddamned prom dress."

Lam incited the rage mob, which descended on the pretty teenager like a flock of vultures. She was called a racist and a cultural appropria-tor, and Buzzfeed added that people thought she couldn't wear the dress because "it was an example of white people adopting customs from a minority culture without experiencing the oppression and discrimination faced by people in that culture."[26]

If the new rule is that we are limited to using or enjoying the artifacts of our self-segregated culture, then everyone who isn't white, English, and gay can get off the Internet (and Alan Turing's family were British colonialists in India). Don't take antibiotics unless you're Scottish. Don't even *think* of celebrating St. Paddy's Day unless you're from the Emerald Isle (the oppressed Irish part of me will feign glorious offense). Don't eat avocado toast unless you're Australian. Don't drink pasteurized milk, get a rabies or anthrax vaccine, or work in microbiology unless you're French. Don't use a home security system or gas mask or play with a Super Soaker or use certain plastics, wood stains, soaps, cosmetics, or medicines unless you are a black American.

Decent people grew outraged at the outrage triggered by Jeremy Lam, so they dug into his Twitter timeline. They discovered tons of racist tweets in which Lam used the N-word (cue "my culture is *not* your slur") and slurred Jews and gays. Daum, for her part, did not bend a knee to the rage mob. She wrote, "To everyone causing so much negativity: I mean no disrespect to the Chinese culture. I'm simply showing my appreciation to their culture. I'm not deleting my post because I've done nothing but show my love for the culture. It's a—dress. And it's beautiful."

First off—every culture appropriates from every other culture, especially in the United States. It's a cultural exchange born of admiration. Is not the point to appreciate other cultures—or would the rage mob prefer segregation and hostility? Rather than get worked up over braids, makeup, jewelry, and clothing, people should feel flattered. An eighteen-year-old white girl in Utah thought a Chinese-style dress was so beautiful that she wanted to wear it to her prom.

We live in an era in which one mistake, one indiscretion can ruin your life. Time erases no errors. You can't learn from them and grow out of them. Public shame will haunt you. The mob doesn't care about a person's spiritual or emotional growth. If it did, would it try to inflict lasting pain on its targets? The mob either doesn't believe that a person can transcend his worst moments or doesn't care. The mob isn't interested in redemption

It has no room in its heart for grace. The mob recoils at forgiveness. It wants destruction.

People are happy to join the mob because it means that the mob isn't after them.

It will be—one day, some day. The mob comes for us all. Its success and its longevity depend on whether people stand against it.

Unlike a milkshake duck, the target of the rage mob is never the object of affection or admiration. The mob sees someone, hears someone, or reads someone with whom it disagrees and embarks on a search-and-destroy mission, avoiding substantive debate. If the mob can't find anything offensive in its victim's background, it will make it up.

The mob's rage is righteous, for the purpose is to wash away sin. The mob's tactics are designed to instill fear. Because of fear, dissenters will remain silent. Because of fear, the mob has control. Because the mob has control, grace and redemption are denied because they threaten the mob's influence.

We are all partially to blame for this phenomenon. We tell everything about our lives to strangers on the Internet to win approval—"likes." What's worse, many of us think nothing of handing our children the means through which they can access the information superhighway with minimal instruction, warning, or supervision. In this age, allowing your kids to go online, especially on social media, is like giving them the keys to your car before you teach them how to drive. A moment of recklessness or stupidity—a specialty of adolescence—can wreck their lives ten years down the road. Everything is fair game, even things you did as a child. Google never forgets, and neither does the mob. Twitter is the worst because it intensifies the wokeness, the grievances, the fury, the hate. In a world with no redemption, can we expect to attract people of virtue to serve in public office?

Successful Refutations of the Rage Mob

The nomination of Judge Brett Kavanaugh to the Supreme Court in 2018 raised the prospect that the ruling in *Roe v. Wade* might be overturned by a strengthened conservative majority on the Court, provoking one of the most frenzied rage mobs in recent history.

To understand the rage, you need to understand Kavanaugh's background and whom he had angered by simply doing his job. A member of Ken Starr's team that investigated President Clinton in the late 1990s, Kavanaugh was credited with being the principal author of the explosive Starr Report, which led to the president's impeachment. In his private practice, Kavanaugh worked on the Elian Gonzalez case and advocated for religious liberty.[27] In 2000, he was part of Governor George W. Bush's legal team handling the Florida recount in the presidential election. Later he was an assistant to President Bush, who eventually appointed him to the U.S. Court of Appeals for the District of Columbia. His presumed views on abortion and the Second Amendment troubled the left, which was deeply suspicious of his Catholicism as well.

The revenge campaign to block Kavanaugh's confirmation was brutal. He was portrayed as a dopey but wild and wealthy frat boy who drunkenly exposed himself or, worse, drugged and raped women. His confirmation hearing was so heated, the Democratic senators so rancorous, and the protests so malicious that his wife rushed their daughters out of the room on the first day.[28] When she returned to watch her husband fight for his life, the press excoriated her.

Democratic senators and the press fawned over Christine Blasey Ford, the accuser who contradicted her own testimony and slammed Leland Keyser, her "best friend," who refused to corroborate her story despite bullying by Ford's lawyers and supporters.[29] The #MeToo champ Dianne Feinstein ignored Ford's story until it was politically advantageous.

For the mob to be successful, the target cannot fight back, and the target cannot have allies.

Kavanaugh's highly anticipated opening statement was a watershed moment. His nomination in the balance, he showed Senate Republicans how much fight he had in him. Had he failed to defend himself, Trump might have been disinclined to fight as well. Had he been too belligerent,

Kavanaugh would have looked like the antagonist. Had he been too soft, the rage mob would have appeared unbeatable. He fired a salvo that knocked the rage mob back on its heels, portraying himself as a husband, a father, a human being dragged through the mud on false charges. He defended not only himself but his marriage and family as well—everything the left wanted to swallow whole along with his nomination:

> The day after the allegation appeared, I told this committee that I wanted a hearing as soon as possible to clear my name. I demanded a hearing for the very next day. Unfortunately, it took the committee ten days to get to this hearing. In those ten long days, as was predictable and as I predicted, my family and my name have been totally and permanently destroyed by vicious and false additional accusations. The ten-day delay has been harmful to me and my family, to the Supreme Court and to the country. When this allegation first arose, I welcomed any kind of investigation. Senate, F. B. I. or otherwise. The committee now has conducted a thorough investigation, and I've cooperated fully....
>
> Since my nomination in July, there's been a frenzy on the left to come up with something, anything to block my confirmation. Shortly after I was nominated, the Democratic Senate leader said he would "oppose me with everything he's got." A Democratic senator on this committee publicly referred to me as evil. Evil. Think about that word. And said that those that supported me were "complicit and evil." Another Democratic senator on this committee said, "Judge Kavanaugh is your worst nightmare." A former head of the Democratic National Committee said, "Judge Kavanaugh will threaten the lives of millions of Americans for decades to come."
>
> I understand the passions of the moment. But I would say to those senators: Your words have meaning. Millions of Americans listened carefully to you. Given comments like those, is it any surprise that people have been willing to do

anything, to make any physical threat against my family? To send any violent email to my wife, to make any kind of allegation against me, and against my friends, to blow me up and take me down?

You sowed the wind for decades to come. I fear that the whole country will reap the whirlwinds. The behavior of several of the Democratic members of this committee at my hearing a few weeks ago was an embarrassment.

Kavanaugh was far from done.

This confirmation process has become a national disgrace. The Constitution gives the Senate an important role in the confirmation process, but you have replaced advise and consent with search and destroy....

This is a circus. The consequences will extend long past my nomination. The consequences will be with us for decades. This grotesque and coordinated character assassination will dissuade confident and good people of all political persuasions from serving our country. And as we all know in the United States political system of the early 2000s, what goes around comes around....

I will not be intimidated into withdrawing from this process. You have tried hard. You've given it your all. No one can question your efforts. Your coordinated and well-funded efforts to destroy my good name and destroy my family will not drag me out. The vile threats of violence against my family will not drive me out. You may defeat me in the final vote, but you'll never get me to quit.

Never.

I watched his remarks live. Somehow during the course of his statement I went from being seated to standing. Callers flooded the phones on my nationally syndicated radio program that day and for the next solid week with a newfound energy. This one man's fight represented everyman's fight. Kavanaugh's righteously blistering opening statement, his defiance of the rage mob, his daring the Democrats to do their worst were the cue Republicans were waiting for, and into the breach they went.

Senator Lindsey Graham, the warrior the Senate needed at that moment, devoted his allotted time not to questioning Kavanaugh but to taking his fellow senators to task:

> Boy, you [Democrats] all want power. God, I hope you never get it. I hope the American people can see through this sham. That you knew about it and you held it. You had no intention of protecting Dr. Ford. None....
>
> She's as much of a victim as you are. God, I hate to say it because these have been my friends, but let me tell you, when it comes to this, you're looking for a fair process, you came to the wrong town at the wrong time, my friend....
>
> To my Republican colleagues, if you vote no, you're legitimizing the most despicable thing I have seen in my time in politics.

To add insult to injury, progress pundits tried to shame Kavanaugh for fighting back, though most conservatives were not having any of it.

No one can forget the powerful image of a righteously angry Brett Kavanaugh refusing to bow to the rage mob, his wife seated behind him, her pained expression a mixture of anger, pride, and fear.

In that moment the Democrats failed to realize that they had overplayed their hand. Keelhauling the nominee pleased their base, but much of the public was appalled, as it made clear in the election that soon followed.

By subjecting Brett Kavanaugh to such an ugly ordeal, the left turned many voters—not just Republicans, but independents and even Democrats—into Ashley Kavanaugh. Women across the country put themselves into Mrs. Kavanaugh's shoes. What if *my* husband were wrongly accused? My son? My brother? My friend?

A wife and mother, I wondered the same thing myself. Was there no presumption of innocence until evidence provided proof of guilt? If an appointment to the Supreme Court could be thwarted by false accusations, what happens when the attacks do not draw national attention? If there is no hope for justice at that level, there is no hope of justice at any level.

It wasn't just women who were affected by the mob's attacks. The Kavanaugh witch hunt shook the confidence of many men, young and old, in our political system. Much as the Clarence Thomas hearings flipped the political switch of my late friend Andrew Breitbart, so the Kavanaugh hearing emboldened a new generation of young men.

Voters were infuriated. The media used the phrase "Kavanaugh fallout" to describe the growing animus of voters against politicians who contributed to the effort to humiliate and destroy an innocent man and his family.

The Kavanaugh confirmation vote became the litmus test for every Democrat and Republican on the ballot across the country and propelled Republican voter enthusiasm. Trump's approval moved up, with a *Wall Street Journal*–NBC poll giving him the best rating of his presidency to that time, at 47/49.[30] Senator Joe Manchin of West Virginia, the lone Democrat to vote in favor of confirming Kavanaugh, almost certainly saved his reelection with his vote.[31]

The rage mob's witch hunt affected the #MeToo movement's credibility too. As recently as November 2017, according to one poll, 80 percent of Republican men were inclined to believe a woman who claimed to be a victim of sexual assault. After the "evidence-free, politically charged, and eleventh-hour hearings to litigate the culpability of Supreme Court Justice Brett Kavanaugh," that figure had dropped to 21 percent.[32]

This wasn't just a fight for SCOTUS, it was also the second major refutation of the rage mob.

Not only was Kavanaugh confirmed, but the expected "blue wave" in the 2018 elections was considerably diminished. Republicans lost the

House of Representatives but increased their majority in the Senate—
almost certainly because of Kavanaugh. The rage mob was not invincible
after all.

Kavanaugh fought back in a way Republicans never do but need to
do. He fought for himself and he fought to uphold the integrity of the
nomination process. Those who protected him with equal fierceness were
rewarded. Trump saw the fight in the nominee and gave him further
shade by inviting some of the arrows to himself. That act of defiance by
Kavanaugh, his refusal to be crucified by ideologues, inspired a new
"resistance" of sorts among the Republican Party, conservatives, independents, and libertarians. It was a disastrous gamble for the Democrats,
and the effects will still be measurable in more ways than one for years
to come.

Kavanaugh offered one of the more recent refutations of the rage
mob, but the first one came from Chick-fil-A.

Dan Cathy, the owner of the hugely popular chicken sandwich chain,
is a Christian who lives his faith, never hiding it to gain favor with the
world. In July 2012, a Christian publication asked him about his views
on same-sex marriage, a subject that has roiled this country for two
decades, and the company's support for the traditional family:

> "Well, guilty as charged," said Cathy when asked about this
> opposition.
>
> "We are very much supportive of the family—the biblical
> definition of the family unit. We are a family-owned business,
> a family-led business, and we are married to our first wives.
> We give God thanks for that.
>
> "We operate as a family business ... our restaurants are
> typically led by families—some are single. We want to do
> anything we possibly can to strengthen families. We are very
> much committed to that," Cathy emphasized.
>
> "We intend to stay the course. We know that it might not
> be popular with everyone, but thank the Lord, we live in a

country where we can share our values and operate on biblical principles."[33]

Soon it was reported that Cathy and his family's charitable arm, the Winshape Foundation, donated to Christian-based groups like the Fellowship of Christian Athletes. Because such groups are faith-based and promote traditional marriage, the left labeled them "anti-gay," a disingenuous term that implies active hostility.

LGBT activists and social justice warriors were aghast. Cathy wasn't using the restaurants' registers as pulpits or imposing his perspective on any employee or customer. He was simply asked about his personal beliefs and he shared them. In fact, Chick-fil-A proudly employs both gay and straight staff and serves all. The closest the Cathy family comes to imposing its beliefs on anyone is its insistence on the unfailingly polite service that Chick-fil-A customers enjoy. That wasn't enough for the activists, the social justice worries, the rage mob. Cathy's "wrong" opinion about the meaning of human sexuality was all the justification they needed to launch a national boycott of the restaurant chain—a boycott that imperiled the jobs of Chick-fil-A employees both gay and straight.

Chick-fil-A's customers around the country organized to patronize the business on the day the boycott was to begin, showcasing support for the business, the Cathy family, faith, and tolerance. I took my children to our local Chick-fil-A. It was summer, and the car line was forty-five minutes long. Despite the heat and the crowds, the employees were smiling and always responded, "My pleasure." According to press coverage, the scene at our local restaurant wasn't an anomaly; it was the same with every Chick-fil-A restaurant across the nation.

Dan Cathy didn't bend a knee to the rage mob. He didn't capitulate, he didn't surrender his faith or his belief or his free exercise of thought. Cathy forfeited nothing, he gave up nothing, he surrendered nothing. Cathy's dual defense of faith and free thought was as powerful and successful as any in modern Christian and conservative history. He did it without a cross word, without violence, without political operatives, without staged PR and social media bots, or anything else. I believe that we are meant to live our lives in such a way that we evangelize without evangelizing, that our actions and stewardship of others cause people to question their lack of faith or their lack of ethics, morals, integrity. Cathy and Chick-fil-A didn't respond to the hate with hate.

One recorded exchange from this national boycott went viral, and the reaction of the Chick-fil-A employee planted a seed in my heart. A tactic of the national boycott was to visit Chick-fil-A and order nothing but demand a free large water. If denied, the boycotter was to cite Proverbs 25:21: "If your enemy is hungry, give him food to eat; if he is thirsty, give him water to drink." Reciting Bible verses to own the cons! Adam Smith videoed himself doing just that at a Chick-fil-A in Tucson. The target of his abuse, an employee named Rachel, bore it with a pleasant and loving demeanor, telling Smith that the company served and valued all people. As he continued to harangue her, she winced but maintained her kind expression. Smith got his water, left the store, and uploaded his video on YouTube. Bad idea.

Instead of receiving accolades, Smith provoked a terrific backlash. Internet sleuths identified him and informed his employer. His name and behavior made it into the press. He apologized, but it was too late. He lost his job and was condemned by the right and by many on the left. Unable to get another job, he reportedly ended up on food stamps.

At first, Smith seemed not to understand that the uproar wasn't over what he was fighting for but how he was fighting. He recorded another video of himself, this time apologizing to Rachel, who did not want her last name to be publicized: "Rachel, I'm sorry for treating you so inhumanely. I compromised my personal integrity. While I might not agree with everyone's views, I always want to treat the other person with respect. I did not do that with you."

It didn't matter to the rage mob—and this particular mob was conservative.

I can't point fingers. I was one of them. I joined in joyfully celebrating this man's very public fall. Headlines mocked him for being on food stamps. It was *schadenfreude*. In reality, we became him.

Rachel granted one and only one interview, to Fox Business with Stuart Varney, substituting for Neil Cavuto that day. She appeared with her fiancé, who sat silently by her side for support. Varney asked if she forgave Smith. "I do forgive Adam Smith. I think he realizes how bad of a decision it was for him to make that tape. I feel really sorry for him and his family. … It's not about Chick-fil-A, it's but how one human being should treat another," said Rachel. "I'm really glad that I could be an example of how we should serve each other," she added, noting that Smith's quarrel was with the corporation, not its employees, but "most people don't make that distinction."

Rachel attributed her response to Smith's provocation to her "training and the upbringing I had." Asked if she was tempted to "give back as good as she got," Rachel replied, "Oh sure, he was looking for me to react poorly. It's not my personality, I would never do anything hateful in return to someone." Varney praised her to which she humbly replied: "I'm just a service worker doing my job." She ended with a response to Smith: "I forgive you. I really hope that America will forgive you and treat you with the respect that I chose to treat you with that day."

Smith wanted a bad reaction, and Rachel didn't give him one. She didn't, but many across America did. Who do you think left a deeper impression on Smith's heart? The angry doxxers who hunted him down and exposed him after his cruel behavior? Or Rachel, "just a service worker," whose response brimmed with strength and compassion? This is not to say that Smith didn't deserve much of the harsh criticism he received. He was publicly scorched. Spiritual growth can come from being humbled in the same way that controlled burns improve the health of a field. It benefitted Smith spiritually, but it did go too far. Many of us missed a valuable lesson in Rachel and Adam Smith's exchange. In our zeal to see someone "get his" for an act of cruelty, we became more like Adam Smith in our response instead of becoming more like Rachel, who provided an example for a divided nation to emulate. She's a service worker in more ways than one.

Chick-fil-A provided the first major refutation of the rage mob, but later it made one of biggest surrenders.

In recent years the company has faced opposition while trying to expand internationally. Its first British location closed because of protests[34] over its Christian associations. In the United States, the cities of Buffalo[35] and San Antonio[36] kept Chick-fil-A out of their airports because of the company's "legacy of anti-LGBTQ behavior."[37] The company's enemies finally drew blood in 2019, and Chick-fil-A announced changes in the Winshape Foundation's giving. The president of Chick-fil-A, Tim Tassopoulos, told the press, "There's no question we know that, as we go into new markets, we need to be clear about who we are. There are lots of articles and newscasts about Chick-fil-A, and we thought we needed to be clear about our message."[38]

If by distancing itself from groups like the Salvation Army and FCA, Chick-fil-A is attempting to project a "we're not that type of Christian" message, it is only confirming the smears from which it was steadfastly defended by Christians who are left wondering how the company itself sees them.

Some listeners asked me if I was going to boycott the restaurant. I'm not particularly keen on such hive-mind actions, and I don't think that evangelism begins or ends with a fast food chicken restaurant. I know some feel betrayed by a company they went out of their way to support in the face of cultural attacks. I also know that those lamenting Chick-fil-A's decision to stop associating with the Salvation Army will increase their own donations. They will answer that call of need just as they answered the call to defend faith-based business seven years ago.

Here's a truth we need to remember: Christians in culture need to stop looking to any other savior but Jesus. The battle has already been won. Never forget this. Also never forget: Chick-fil-A choosing to bend a knee to the rage mob doesn't erase the victory Christians across the country won repeatedly against cancel culture. We didn't cede this victory to the mob, Chick-fil-A did. When Christians stand up—be it for Duck Dynasty, The Passion of the Christ, or the beliefs of people who sell chicken sandwiches, we win. Chick-fil-A's retreat does not erase what Rachel did.

In a world of Adam Smiths, be a Rachel.

That is the grace we should emulate if we want to cancel rage mobs and the cancel culture.

CHAPTER SIX

The Death of Redemption

"Now there is a final reason I think that Jesus says, 'Love your enemies.' It is this: that love has within it a redemptive power. And there is a power there that eventually transforms individuals."

—Martin Luther King, Jr.

Fake stewardship—pretending to care for one's fellow man—has become a cottage industry. Despite their carefully crafted veneer of compassion and concern, piety-spouting politicians and celebrities often think and feel the opposite. Tyrants arrive clothed in synthetic virtue, exhorting the masses to care for one another while outsourcing their own stewardship. Time spent on any effort that isn't politically rewarded is time wasted.

Even atoning for one's sins is outsourced these days. Joining a rage mob is as easy as joining a gym. Make the other guy pay for his transgressions thrice over, and you can feel better about your own sin. In the past, you wouldn't excommunicate a friend or family member over a difference of opinion. Today, if someone told a bad joke ten years ago, his family, his reputation, and his life's work are forfeit. The mob demands an apology, which the terrified offender usually offers readily, but it's nothing more than his last words before the executioner's swing. Instead of responding to character failings, however trivial, with genuine concern and perhaps a prayer or good wishes, people respond *gleefully* to the discovery of any flaw, especially in the political realm. It is a harsh landscape void of redemption and reconciliation.

This book began to germinate in my mind when I read an interview with Norm Macdonald. The comedian. Yes, the dry, hysterical Burt Reynolds impersonator who once told the longest, most ridiculously hilarious joke (it was about a moth) I've ever heard on an episode of Conan O'Brien's late-night show. I don't know why, but I'm always surprised when comedians get serious on a topic, or speak sense over absurdity. I feel like it's a temperature reading: When the comedians get serious about something, then it's time to worry—like when the creatures in the woods hush upon sensing an approaching predator.

Asked about the dismissal of Roseanne Barr, who gave Macdonald his first break in Hollywood, from her new television show, he said:

> The model used to be: admit wrongdoing, show complete contrition and then we give you a second chance. Now it's admit wrongdoing and you're finished. And so the only way to survive is to deny, deny, deny. That's not healthy—that there is no forgiveness. I do think that at some point it will end with a completely innocent person of prominence sticking a gun in his head and ending it. That's my guess. I know a couple of people [Louis C. K. and Roseanne Barr] this has happened to.[1]

He was exactly right.

Macdonald also defended Jimmy Fallon for having Donald Trump as a guest on *The Tonight Show*:

> He is just all about fun and silliness. That's what his audience wants. And then to be maligned for "humanizing" Trump. Funny, I thought he was a human. If you have the nominee to be president on your show and he is your guest, then he is

your guest. Don't have him on the show if you don't want him.

In a subsequent interview with Howard Stern, Macdonald said, "You'd have to have Down syndrome to not feel sorry" for #MeToo victims. For all of this, Macdonald's appearance on *The Tonight Show* with Jimmy Fallon was canceled.[2] He later tweeted, "Roseanne and Louis have both been very good friends of mine for many years. They both made terrible mistakes and I would never defend their actions. If my words sounded like I was minimizing the pain that their victims feel to this day, I am deeply sorry."

Later that week, an emotionally tarred-and-feathered Macdonald faced the women of *The View*. The usually quick-witted comedian was obviously contrite—slower to speak than usual, and so soft-spoken as to be almost inaudible. He explained how, when speaking to Stern, he was looking for a hyperbolic way to say "stupid," and, as he said, almost used a word from the past that used to be acceptable before stopping himself and grabbing the weak reed of another word that was just as unpalatable. The women joked that he seemed scared to say anything, noting that comedy is dying because of political correctness. As Macdonald again acknowledged that his Down syndrome remark was "wrong and insensitive," Joy Behar needled him, adding "and stupid," before Whoopi Goldberg jumped in: "As comics, we've all stepped in it."

"Thanks for coming to us and talking to us about this," said Goldberg.

"Well, I hope that I didn't offend any of you guys," Macdonald said softly, not looking up from the table. There was a heavily awkward pause before Joy Behar said, "Not at all." Goldberg kept the segment moving and teased Macdonald's show for him as they wrapped the discussion.

I've been a fan of Macdonald's since I was a kid, having seen virtually everything he has done, including projects for which he simply wrote. Macdonald is one of the most underappreciated comics ever and is incredibly smart. Sometimes he flies over the heads of those less familiar with his work. Sometimes I think he plans it this way. I had wondered if this interview was one of those times. I wasn't sure. Macdonald is no pushover. Whatever was percolating inside his head, his answers and demeanor were further inspiration for me to write this book.

Why does it seem most people in politics and pop culture are against redemption? Why don't people want to allow others a redemptive path? Because no one can apologize, and no one can forgive. But forgive what, exactly?

"Forgiveness sets the stage for peace rather than payback," writes Tom Gilson, an author and senior editor of *The Stream*.[3] But everything in today's culture encourages the opposite. Macdonald is a prophet, because the rage mob came for him after his interview was published. They were mad over his brief remark concerning the #MeToo movement:

> I'm happy the #MeToo movement has slowed down a little bit. It used to be, "One hundred women can't be lying." And then it became, "One woman can't lie." And that became, "I believe all women." And then you're like, "What?" Like, that Chris Hardwick guy I really thought got the blunt end of the stick there.

Gilson writes "You can't get to forgiveness without having something actually wrong to forgive."[4] Today, people are condemned for simply holding the wrong view, being the wrong color, or being the wrong sex. They're wrong for being what they are. Shaming is a favorite tactic of the rage mob, a tactic of control, a power play to avoid discussion. Gilson writes:

> Strategies that depend on shaming depend on power—social power, that is, but power nonetheless. Which is bad enough to begin with, but it gets even worse than that. Shaming shortcuts thinking, too. We run into deep trouble when we

make the other side's position unthinkable, but the flip side is just as bad. We make our own position unthinkable, too, though in a different sense: Questioning ourselves becomes unthinkable. You don't need to think. You just do.

American political culture absolutely depends on thought, reflection, deliberation. That's quickly being replaced with power plays, of which shaming may be the most effective currently in use. . . . Shaming is becoming our favored method for dealing with wrongs, whether real or perceived.

There is no forgiveness anymore because forgiveness is not politically expedient. Forgiving someone is like giving away a wild card in Uno. Forgiveness has been twisted into acceptance, surrender, even tolerance. If someone apologizes and is forgiven, then healing can begin and peace can be achieved. But such an occurrence may be catching. And people might notice that there *is* life after political disagreements, that people of different ideological persuasions can still make peace and live civilly. When a person is humanized by being forgiven, it becomes harder to sell a message of division.

So what's the point of apologizing? No one is going to forgive you. What is the point of forgiving if no one apologizes? As if an apology were required for forgiveness.

Apologies and forgiveness are political seppuku. Forgiveness is for people who can be rehabilitated from the sickness of their wrongs and reintegrated into society. Society accepts you as long as you replace everything you are with everything it is. Unfortunately, "wrongthink" is an unforgivable sin, one that no amount of groveling, apologies, or excuses will redeem. There is no hope of peace because forgiveness isn't an option. The only acceptable response is destruction, which denies redemption while acknowledging that the purpose was never about changing hearts and minds but destroying any challenges to power. It's not even about the truth of a particular matter. It's about power. It's only ever been about power. The truth is irrelevant. It's difficult to find common ground when we can't even agree upon certain truths, but that doesn't mean we can't live civilly with one another.

I think people *want* to be reconciled to one another, but no one is willing to humble himself to the point of doing so. People are worried about image, about the personal capital it will cost them to commit such an act. Around the time of the Macdonald controversy, Sean Spicer announced he was going to be on *Dancing with the Stars*, and Fox News hired Sarah Huckabee Sanders as its newest contributor. The rage mob once again grabbed the torches and pitchforks. CNN pundits condemned Sanders's hire while hurriedly making a place for their newest contributor, Andrew McCabe, who was waiting to learn if he would be indicted for perjury. (Crime pays, kids!)

The hires irked Jennifer Rubin, a cantankerous Democrat who still identifies as a "conservative," lest cable news have no use for her bitter, unoriginal commentary. She sneered on MSNBC: "What we should be doing is shunning these people. Shunning, shaming these people is a statement of moral indignation that these people are not fit for polite society. I think it's absolutely abhorrent that any institution of higher learning, any news organization, or any entertainment organization that has a news outlet would hire these people." She added: "We have to level them because if there are survivors, if there are people who weather this storm, they will do it again. They will take this as confirmation that, 'Hey, it just pays to ride the waves—look at me, I've made it through.'"[5]

Because Sanders and Spicer think differently than Rubin, they should be "shunned and shamed." Rubin and those like her are careful to avoid defining their shifting moral standards. If they did, they'd have to justify their indignation. For many of them, their indignation isn't over an abandonment of principles within the GOP. They carved out a niche for themselves by opposing a political shift. When the shift happened, their influence was downsized and they became essentially NPCs (non-player characters) in Republican and conservative politics.

Kyle Kashuv, a very bright eighteen-year-old, was admitted to Harvard. When he was sixteen, he had the bad sense to be in a pretty nasty text group, and Kashuv wrote some pretty nasty things. He used the N-word about a frillion times, and he made disparaging remarks about Jews (he's Jewish himself). Kashuv grew out of that, but he held retrograde views on gun rights, and two years later (which is a very long time in the life of a teenager), one of his friends showed some of those old texts to some journalists who had nothing better to do than report on the putrid rants of sixteen-year-olds.

Kashuv apologized with genuine sincerity, asking to be judged on who he is now, not who he was—but that wasn't enough. The adults wanted him to suffer. They petitioned Harvard, whose student body is apparently unsullied by sin, to rescind Kashuv's acceptance, and the university obliged. It was too late for Kashuv to apply to another university or to search for scholarships. To be fair, Harvard had previously withdrawn acceptances for similar behavior—and even disinvited the traitor Chelsea Manning. It is well within the university's right to bow to the rage mob, but that doesn't make it the appropriate punishment.

The strength of any rule is consistency. Harvard never condemned the racial appropriation of its own Senator Pochahonky, Elizabeth Warren, who for years passed herself off as a person of color as she pursued a career that eventually took her to Harvard Law School. Virgina's governor, Blackface Abort'em, also known as Ralph Northam, wore blackface so often in college that his friends called him "Coonman." He admitted to being in racist yearbook photos during an awkward press conference in which he also admitted to wearing blackface while dressing as Michael Jackson, offering to demonstrate his moonwalk for the assembled reporters. The world was deprived of this delightful potential gif only by his quick-thinking wife, who interceded with a firm "no."

Northam can skin-walk as a collegiate and all is forgiven, bless his redemptive arc! But Kashuv? The Jewish conserva-teen who wrote stupid and ignorant things a couple of years ago? *He* must be made an example.

Forgiveness. Redemption. A comeback. America used to love comeback stories. They're a Hollywood standby. We cheer them because we hope we might make one ourselves someday. We know what it feels like to struggle, to miss opportunities, to make mistakes. We know the feeling of looking up in despair and finding a friendly face and extended hand. We know the fulfillment that comes with reconciliation. It's a prodigal son feeling, the tinge of bittersweet regret mixed with joy.

The left hates people, the right hates ideology. To the left, the issues anthropomorphize into people. They cannot separate the person from the issue, the soul from the stance.

I know what you're thinking: *You're Dana Loesch. You said the media love the ratings that come from tragedy. You held up an hourglass in a promo for your program on NRATV and announced, "Time's up."*

Yes. And many overreacted.

There is a time and place for righteous indignation. Lately there has been too little righteous indignation. In its place is outrage—raw, tactical outrage.

We're supposed to be the good guys. We are supposed to hold the measure of "moral betters." I was naive to believe that there was an exception to the adage "absolute power corrupts absolutely," that one side could remain untouched by the corruption of absolute power. There is a difference, though, between how the left and the right respond to corruption. The left is unashamed of its corruption and believes that the ends justifies the means. The right pretends its square, churchy, old-fashioned American veneer protects it from any suspicion of corruption. The right doesn't care *privately* while pretending to care publicly.

My optimistic naiveté died in the spring of 2019 when it became undeniable that even the supposed champions of truth, justice, and liberty were infested with greed and malice and were hostile to transparency. It was like discovering that Santa Claus was nothing more than a tool of nostalgia and behavioral control—but the nihilistic atom bomb version, fifteen tons of Santa disbelief.

We are supposed to be the good guys.

And yet we're not.

At best, we're the *better* guys.

How can you keep faith alive when goodness seems scarce?

The first thing you can do is to stop looking to your fellow man to be an exemplar of goodness. You will always be disappointed. You will always feel discouraged if you look to your right and to your left as your measure of morality.

To stop the outrage cycle, you must first disempower those operating the divisive wokescold industry by refusing to indulge it any longer. You must believe people when they are genuinely contrite. Otherwise, again, what is the point?

Kevin Hart, a comedian who has made homophobic jokes in the past, told Ellen DeGeneres, "I'm kinda upset, because these ten years are being ignored, they're being brushed past. No headlines are saying 'Ten years ago, he apologized.'" Hart explained how during many movie junkets promoting his films he had apologized, repeatedly, saying he used to make jokes like that for laughs, but he's grown and "doesn't do that anymore."

For years Hart apologized, but it was never good enough. How do you expect to convince people of the importance of apologies when you refuse to accept them?

A black sixth-grade girl in Virginia told her family and the public that three white students had held her down on the playground at school and cut her dreadlocks. Her school, Immanuel Christian School, was of particular interest to the media because the Second Lady, Karen Pence, teaches there part-time. In a tearful interview with the local press, the girl described in detail how the boys held her down and put a hand over her mouth, calling her "ugly" and her hair "nappy." Her mother complained that the school wasn't doing enough.

A couple of days later, the family issued a statement. The child had made up the story. In perhaps one of the most heartfelt apologies I've ever read, the family stated:

> To those young boys and their parents, we sincerely apologize
> for the pain and anxiety these allegations have caused. To the

administrators and families of Immanuel Christian School, we are sorry for the damage this incident has done to trust within the school family and the undue scorn it has brought to the school. To the broader community, who rallied in such passionate support for our daughter, we apologize for betraying your trust. We understand there will be consequences, and we're prepared to take responsibility for them. We know that it will take time to heal, and we hope and pray that the boys, their families, the school and the broader community will be able to forgive us in time.[6]

When famous actors are staging racial attacks on themselves to boost their careers and certified "victimhood" is the most coveted status, how hard is it to imagine that a child might fabricate such a story? This family appreciated the damage their daughter's lie inflicted, and they met it head-on, no excuses, strongly stating they know there will be consequences and they're prepared to accept the responsibility. *Responsibility!* What a quaint concept it now seems. I hope this family is given the grace it deserves. I hope the media will retract the story as zealously as they reported and exploited it to settle political scores. I'm not holding my breath, but this is a learning experience for many.

Mika Brzezinski, who hates my guts, called Mike Pompeo a "wannabe dictator's butt boy." The outrage peaked and Brzezinski apologized.[7] To her credit, she didn't apologize "if I've offended anyone." She made her amends straight out: "Please allow me to say this face to face. . . . The term is crass and offensive and I apologize to everybody, especially the LGBTQ community and to my colleagues. I just wanted to say on camera, looking people straight in the eye: I am really, really sorry."

Are we so good that we can't accept her apology? Are we to lord it over her in perpetuity, as if to say, "You'll never be better than this"? Sure, it may feel satisfying for a while to get your digs in, but after that feeling fades away, what has it accomplished? Have we demonstrated the grace we seek by those actions?

Redemption is tough, and people don't like to offer it. It's the part of politics we don't discuss because we don't want to give up any advantage on the political battlefield. *Ideas* are what should be battled. If we demand moral perfection, then no one is qualified to shape or discuss our country's policies and future. But if we give each other a break when we foul, maybe, just maybe, we can start the long journey back to a place of civility.

I did this once for Keith Olbermann, a man I dislike greatly, while he was at MSNBC hosting a political opinion show. News broke that he had donated money to Democratic candidates in violation of an MSNBC policy intended to foster an image of bipartisanship. Olbermann was suspended. I publicly countered that the rule was ridiculous considering that Olbermann said things on his program that achieved a level of partisanship and mean-spiritedness that no donation could match. When he was reinstated, he thanked me on air for defending him, adding that he wasn't sure if he would have done the same.

I don't need a quid pro quo. If we offer grace only to the extent it is offered to us, we won't get anywhere.

David Koch, the libertarian billionaire, passed away in August 2019. Despite spending billions of dollars on education,[8] the arts,[9] and medical research,[10] he was loathed by the left and denounced for spending a fraction of what he donated to charity on the campaign to defeat Barack Obama. Any goodwill Koch demonstrated during his life was vitiated by his political views. Hollywood celebrities and progressive pundits celebrated his death. Slate writer Jordan Weissmann tweeted, "I don't believe in an afterlife, but if there is one, I hope his soul suffers for an eternity,"[11] while the actor Ron Perlman tweeted, "Wishing the Koch brothers a speedy reunion."

The nastiness demonstrated by so many in Hollywood and politics provided another glimpse at the awful toll the lack of grace takes on our souls. The left could not forgive Koch the sin of his political affiliation. They ignored his charity, charging that the only reason he donated to cancer research was because he had cancer. The patients seeking treatment in the buildings whose construction he financed, and who were cared for by medical professionals using the latest technology that he paid for, might have had a different view of David Koch. Yes, he wanted to cure a disease that he had—and many are grateful that he was inspired to act in such a way. The only ones whose intentions were petty were those who maligned the great philanthropist.

I sometimes wonder if it's harder for those who have been denied grace to offer it themselves. If you believe in the God of grace, then you know that the measure by which you bestow grace on others is the measure by which you will receive it.

One of the most powerful examples of this occurred in the fall of 2019 at the sentencing of Dallas police officer Amber Guyger, who was convicted of murder after she went home to the wrong apartment and shot dead Botham Jean.[12] Brandt Jean, Botham's brother, publicly forgave his brother's murderer and asked to hug her in the courtroom. I wasn't at the trial, I didn't hear every argument made by the defense, and I won't pretend to understand the sentencing. All I know is that every now and then there comes along a person who lives his faith so fiercely, who loves so courageously, that it stops me in my tracks and makes me evaluate where I am lacking in my own life of faith. I can't imagine the pain that family feels, but I can imagine Botham's joy in Heaven as he watches his brother Brandt show the world what it is to be *of the kingdom* and not of the world. It is *lived*, not compelled. If Brandt Jean can firgive this much, who are we to hold petty grudges?

CHAPTER SEVEN

The Media's Role

"The only thing that kept me alive was the desire
to purge my character."

—*Annie Oakley, on her libel suits against Hearst Newspapers,*
in which she settled or won fifty-four of fifty-five suits

I knew what I was walking into. I got word on a Tuesday that I was to be in Parkland, Florida, the following evening to participate in a CNN-hosted town hall featuring survivors of the massacre at Marjory Stoneman Douglas High School, their families, and area residents. It was not my choice to go, but members of the National Rifle Association and countless others—most of them parents themselves—were worried about how CNN would depict law-abiding gun owners and wanted someone to represent us.

My flight took off in the middle of a thunderstorm. The plane bobbed and weaved among the thick gray clouds as it clawed to thirty thousand feet. I looked out of the window and prayed. That was the extent of my prep: I spent the entire two-and-a-half-hour flight in a deep, uncompromising prayer. I knew I was going from one storm straight into another, where wounds were fresh and hearts were shattered.

CNN treated the town hall as if it were a professional wrestling match. I was once a CNN contributor, and I think highly of many people there, but I had a feeling I was being ambushed. The producers, one of whom I'd known for years, were kind and preemptively apologetic. I think there was genuine worry that I wouldn't appear on the stage. When we got to the venue, I was led to a private greenroom (everyone who would be on stage had his own). The producers briefed me on what would happen, and I learned that I would be seated next to Sheriff Scott Israel of Broward County. So I was to be pitted against a representative of law enforcement officers, who traditionally support the NRA. I assumed that this sheriff, whom I had never met, would be hostile. He showed up flanked by producers, with a coterie of deputies several paces behind him. I walked out into the hall and introduced myself, hoping to get a sense of his disposition toward me.

"Sheriff, my name is Dana Loesch. I want you to know that I am praying for this community and for your and your deputies' guidance," I said with complete sincerity.

Israel was taken aback. Putting out his hand he responded, "Thank you so much. Great to meet you. You know, no hard feelings at all, none at all."

"Yes," I replied slowly, somewhat bewildered. "I understand we are to be on stage together. I hope we can have a good discussion. Nice to meet you, Sheriff."

"Oh absolutely," he replied. "I'll see you up there."

In that brief meeting, the sheriff had shown me his cards. He was planning to lay the blame for the Parkland massacre at my feet. Minutes later, CNN allowed him to take the stage and address the crowded auditorium. He laid into the NRA and referred to me as the "NRA lady," spending a good twenty minutes electioneering and stirring up a crowd whose emotions were already raw. This was the opening act.

Meanwhile, Jake Tapper entered my room to say hello. I've known Jake for several years and find him to be fairer than most because he, unlike others, makes the effort. He and I seemed to realize something simultaneously, unspoken: The night wasn't about winning a debate. It was about simply holding the line. For me, it was about holding the line for constitutional rights despite being a punching bag for the audience. For him, it was about holding down a broadcast for an hour. Jake intimated that there was already no hope of controlling the crowd that had amassed in the arena. After he left, Jeff Zucker, the president of CNN, stopped by briefly. He thanked me for being there and returned to the hallway for more photos. The mood backstage was incongruous with the pain being amplified in the arena for ratings.

We watched on the television in the greenroom as the program began. Senator Marco Rubio was on first with Senator Bill Nelson and Congressman Ted Deutch, who was intent on testing the limits of civility. Rubio was backed into a corner, inch by inch, before he finally invoked certain long-held truths regarding gun rights. It was a difficult spot for an elected official. If he didn't cave in, he'd be called insensitive. If he did, he'd be blasted by constituents worried about losing their right of self-defense. I knew that if Rubio folded it would be harder for me. He lost control of the room; Tapper lost control of the audience. CNN had no control over anything, and that's just how they wanted it.

People were yelling at me before I even walked into the arena. A production assistant nudged me, my cue to walk to the stage, which was set up like a boxing ring without ropes in the middle of the arena. The booing and hissing followed me all the way down the aisle.

"Murderer!" screamed one woman.

"Hateful bitch!" screamed a man.

Keeping a pleasant expression on my face, I did not look at the ground or the ceiling but looked everyone in the eye. I was not afraid, for I had done nothing wrong. I figured that at some point I would be hit or spat on.

As I approached the rollaway stairs that gave access to the stage, a teenage boy appeared to my right. I don't know what I expected, but I didn't expect him to smile.

"Mrs. Loesch! Mrs. Loesch!" he yelled. I stopped. "Mrs. Loesch, you have to stop them. They're talking about banning everything. They want to ban it all. You have to say something, to stop it."

In the few seconds we faced each other I studied his face. He had kind eyes and a genuinely worried expression. He wore an air force t-shirt.

"Does someone in your family serve?" I asked him.

"Yes ma'am, my brother," he said proudly.

"What is your name?"

"Jalen Martin, ma'am."

I squeezed his hand and walked up the steps. His was the last friendly face I'd see all night.

I did not go in there intending to debate. I did not intend to make light of the horror of the massacre or to fight with children, some of whom were barely older than my oldest. Someone needed to be the adult amid the angry activists and hungrily exploitative politicians. I participated in the town hall because a few million people across the country asked me to, expected me to, and wanted me to be their voice in the conversation. I resolved not to shy away from speaking the truth or defending a right. Many people in that arena were in acute pain. Just a week earlier some of them had lost a child. When they spoke, they were desperate to make a point, to say something that would alleviate their pain and contribute to the efforts that might address a terrible problem. Others, who had not suffered a direct personal loss, were there to inflict as much pain as the law allowed on me or on anyone they held responsible for the attack.

There was no moderation. I didn't blame Jake—what could he do? Controlling the audience and encouraging reasoned discourse were impossible in the circus-like atmosphere the network had deliberately fostered. I won't hold my tongue here; I don't care about being a CNN contributor again, and I don't care if they never invite me back. What the executives did that night was wrong. Tacky and wrong. Tone-deaf and wrong. An emotionless approach to understandably impassioned emotions.

Prior to the cameras going live, Sheriff Scott Israel, the Broward County Public Schools superintendent, Robert Runcie, and others were invited to the stage to give impassioned speeches. Israel electioneered and dodged responsibility, though he well knew, as was later widely reported, that his office had not followed up on numerous calls from the community, even the murderer's own family, who, according to the *Florida Sun Sentinel*, once begged the Broward Sheriff's Office to confiscate his guns. Runcie deflected. The bonfire was ignited before we were even miked.

As the event concluded, I stood to shake Jake's hand and leave. The arena had burst into shouts of "Murderer!" and various expletives. Jake strode over, surveying the arena, and asked if I had an escort.

"You probably need to leave here immediately," he said, concerned.

I saw some people jerking the rollaway stairs, my easy exit off the stage, so I slowly made my way toward them, careful not to appear as though I was running from anything. A woman grabbed my arm as I tried to make my way down the stairs. Two of our detail (I later learned that the third had dashed to the front of the stage as a woman had rushed it and climbed over in an attempt to get to me) linked their arms behind me and physically lifted me off the stairs and out of the scrum. They tried to hurry me, but I refused to rush. It was like the "Walk of Atonement" scene from *Game of Thrones*. As I had done when I came in, I kept my head up and looked at every face, meeting the eyes of every person who screamed "Bitch!" or "Burn her!"

Backstage we were met by producers, including a friend of mine who used to work for ABC. There were no words to fill the awkward emptiness as we quickly walked to our waiting car. "I'm sorry," said one. "You did really well out there."

"This could have, and should have, been handled differently," I said in a restrained tone.

We piled into the SUV and headed to the airport to catch the last flight to D.C., where I was to speak at the Conservative Political Action Conference (CPAC) after Vice President Pence early the next morning. Phones that had been on silent began ringing and pinging with calls, texts, and emails. I looked out the window and watched the traffic. While I'd never compare the experience to the anguish of losing a child or hiding in a classroom hoping to not be shot, it was a sort of collateral trauma.

I don't remember how long it took to get to the airport, but I was jolted back to my surroundings by my husband, who urged me to check my phone. Our seventh-grader, whom I'll call P, had texted me repeatedly. He had watched the entire town hall with his brother, my mother, and some of his brother's friends.

"Are u OK?

"Are u OK?

"MOM R U OK?"

"I'm fine, are you OK?" I responded.

"Why were people so mean? WHY WERE THEY LIKE THAT TO YOU????"

My mom texted me as I responded to P: "I am so proud of you. P is texting you, I don't know if you're on the plane already or not. He's very upset."

"I know," I replied, "I'm texting with him now. Thank you."

P was angry, upset, and in tears. "NO ONE EVEN WANTED TO LISTEN TO YOU WHY DID THEY INVITE YOU IF THEY DIDN'T WANT TO LISTEN TO YOU AND ONLY WANTED TO CALL YOU NAMES AND YELL!!!" he texted. His texts were fast and caps-locked. I called him.

"How you doing?" I asked.

"Well, not good!" he yelled, his little voice choked with emotion. He was on the verge of tears but trying bravely not to cry. "Why did they do that to you? Why did they ask you to go there when they weren't interested in talking and only wanted to scream at you?"

"A lot of people there just went through something tragic. They're hurting and trying to process it. People are hurting and sometimes *hurt* people hurt people. Sometimes it's intentional, other times they just need to vent."

"But why do you have to take it?" he asked, his voice fully cracking now. "Why did it have to be you? Why did they have to yell at the other ones? You didn't do anything wrong."

"Some people don't believe that," I explained. "Some people think that because of what I believe I do bear some responsibility." I was honest with him. I wasn't going to do the dirty work of hiding anybody's misplaced blame.

"Well they're wrong! They're wrong, and that's just stupid!" he yelled.

"Yes, but do you think that you're going to convince any person who is angry that they're wrong by being angry back at them? No. You don't solve anger or hate with anger and hate." I told him that he needed to pray and give it to God tonight.

"I'm going to pray," he said—words I won't ever forget. "I'm going to pray for the families of the kids who aren't here anymore, and I'm going to pray for their parents and their school," he said. "And I'm going to pray that they stop being horrible."

I told him that I would call him in the morning before school. That's when I saw a text from my oldest, a young man of few words: "I love you mom and I'm proud of you. Keep going."

The next day, I learned that my kids had been greeted at school with an outpouring of support from the faculty and their friends. My own mom told me later that throughout the broadcast their friends called or group-texted support or observations about points I'd made or things the sheriff or other participants had said or the behavior of the audience. It eased my heart so much to know that they were surrounded by an amazing, faithful community, and I will be forever grateful to them for covering my kids with love and prayer. I am grateful that the principal and the school's president emailed to check on us and how the national furor was affecting our kids. Local law enforcement increased drive-bys past our house. God love them, we had gotten to know them so well, first after we informed them of "swatting" possibilities (a fake crime report intended to provoke a SWAT team response), and later after a man posted my address, cell phone number, and photos of my home on Twitter and kept calling my home from an unlisted number, threatening to kill me in my front yard. The police came to our home the evening that it happened, and the perpetrator called while the officers stood in my living room. I handed my phone to one of them and let him talk to the officer; when he realized the police were there he hung up. We kept most things of this nature from the kids, but it was harder to be secretive when we told them they couldn't play in the front yard or ride their bikes in the cul-de-sac. We were honest with them about the situation, careful to avoid any exaggeration, and always mentioned our amazing police and neighbors. We assured them that Mom and Dad were trained, equipped, and fully capable of defending the family against anyone who tried to hurt them or get into our house. This put them at ease, as did the love and grace at their school, where I knew they were protected.

Someone once asked me how would I feel knowing my kids were at a school where a teacher had a gun? I reflected back to when we first met with the principal at my children's school, where they were enrolled after being homeschooled.

"What is your school security situation?" I had asked the junior high principal. He informed me that they had a school resource officer, along with volunteer grandparents and parents who are trained and undergo background checks to patrol the school's perimeter.

"Do any of the teachers carry?" I asked flatly.

"Well, yes, being that this is Texas, a number of them do carry, and we know who, what, and when," he laughed. "Also, if it helps to put your mind at ease, I just finished building an AR-15 as well that I keep—" I interrupted him.

"Can I come here, too?"

The flight from Florida landed late in D.C., and we got into another SUV with our detail and made our way to CPAC. I got about four hours of sleep before my speech. My mind continued to replay the mental carousel of faces I saw in the arena the night before—not the angry faces, contorted by rage, screaming epithets at me, but the ones that weren't screaming, the ones lost in the fury and chaos of it all—the families of the kids lost. I remembered one dark-haired woman in particular, who sat to my nine o'clock. Written on her face was an anguish no one should ever have to know. When she rose to speak, the cameras focusing on her shakily unfolding the paper on which she had written her thoughts. She was the picture of raw, exhausted emotion—a mother robbed, a heart ravaged by grief. She didn't yell at me; she didn't talk about gun control. She talked about her child and how much she hurt. When I stood to leave and the arena erupted around me, I saw her in my periphery, staring at the ceiling and sobbing, trying to hold it together. I want to be clear here. The people who were identified as victims' families were in no emotional state to be part of any rage mob that night. They were just trying to get through the event, and for some of them grief made it nearly impossible to speak.

As I gave my CPAC speech—ad libbing most of it, as I usually do—the daze from the previous evening dissipated and I felt anger, but not for the reasons you may think. My mind kept returning to how quickly the cameras focused on a crying mother at the town hall, crassly intruding into her heart, and how CNN had rushed to stage the event just a week after the attack. One of the parents told me a short time later that he was so adrift in despair that night that he could barely process what he was going through.

I couldn't walk anywhere at CPAC without those same cameras appearing from behind every corner. There was always some reporter insinuating through his questions that I and the millions of law-abiding Americans I represented were somehow culpable for what happened at Parkland. All of this swirled in my head as I stood backstage. The contrast between the people who had screamed epithets at me not twenty-four hours before and the people who stood and cheered when I walked on stage was unsettling. "Are we that divided?" I asked myself as I approached the dais. The more I spoke the angrier I became. It was a righteous anger—an anger born of the circumstances, the exploiters, the narrative peddlers. I spotted the cameras at the back of the room, and the mental image of the cameras training on that grieving mother the night before, siphoning off some of her soul-crushing grief for the audience, returned to my mind. In perhaps the most unleashed moment of my career, I spat the uncomfortably true words:

The media loves mass shootings—they don't love the tragedy of it, but they love the ratings. Crying white mothers are ratings gold to you and many of the legacy media in the back. And notice I said crying *white* mothers, because there are thousands of grieving black mothers in Chicago every weekend, and you don't see town halls for them, do you? Where's the CNN town hall for Chicago? Where's the CNN town hall for sanctuary cities? Where was the voice of those junior ROTC members last night, CNN? If it bleeds it leads, but it has to be the right people in the right communities at the right time.

Those who judged my words hadn't seen what I had seen in those past sixteen hours. They didn't see Jeff Zucker glad-handing and posing for photos backstage while grieving parents clutching their notes waited quietly in the arena for the program to begin. They didn't sit through a town hall designed not to reach solutions to a horrific problem but to wring the last bit of emotion from a broken community.

Those who judged and weren't at that Parkland town hall *judged wrongly.*

The rage mob descended, demanding retractions and apologies, feigning outrage when they were culpable. I refused to oblige. I never have and never will.

Let me be clear about my remarks at CPAC that morning: *I apologize for nothing.*

I will not apologize to the portion of the media at which my remarks were aimed, for they recklessly suggested that I and innocent gun owners were responsible for the Parkland massacre. The rage mob, instead of directing its anger toward a television network that exploited anguish for ratings and further divided the country, attacked me for accurately—and politely—pointing it out. Instead of directing its fury at the policy of simply not reporting students' criminal behavior so as to shut off the school-to-prison pipeline—the so-called "Promise Program," which protected the Parkland murderer—the rage mob went after me and law-abiding gun owners. Instead of blasting Superintendent Robert Runcie for failing to protect the staff and students, the rage mob, egged on by irresponsible media coverage, blamed me and law-abiding gun owners.

The rage mob did not want to blame the officials and authorities at Marjory Stoneman Douglas High School who knew that one of their students had a lifelong record of alarming behavior, who knew about his threats to other students and his assault on his adoptive mother, who knew about the repeated calls to the Broward Sheriff's Office. It was more convenient and politically advantageous for the rage mob to blame people who, until that terrible afternoon, had never heard of MSD High School.

Had I been superintendent of Broward County Public Schools, I would have told the bureaucrats of the Department of Education that they could shove their Promise Program where the sun doesn't shine. I would have made sure my school perimeter was locked and that the on-site security staff weren't worthless cowards, and I would have been transparent with parents about the state of our school's security. I would have moved heaven and earth to have the murderer removed from the school and involuntarily committed—which, given his lengthy and terrifying history, should not have been a problem. A program that was supposed to serve as a shield for minority students actually shielded a dangerous white student and enabled him to shoot others, many them minorities.

Had I been the Broward County sheriff, I would have responded to the calls of terrified innocents reporting a schoolmate's assaults and murderous threats. I would have arrested him for his *numerous* digital death threats (under Florida Statute Section 826.10), rendering him ineligible to purchase, carry, or possess a firearm. The problem in Parkland wasn't the existing laws; it was the scandalous failure to enforce them.

With the exception of the *South Florida Sun Sentinel*, the legacy media failed to report any of this. They were too busy smearing me and the NRA. Alisyn Camerota came down harder on me for observing, correctly, that her show allowed me and others to be called "child murderers" than on the guests who made that disgraceful accusation. She wasn't the only one. CNN's Brian Stelter gave David Hogg, a Parkland student who became a media celebrity, a national stage to make scurrilous accusations against me.[1]

Were I running Congress, we'd have national reciprocity, we'd repeal the National Firearms Act and the bump stock rule, and we wouldn't criminalize legal, private transfers of firearms that are already regulated.

If I didn't care about children, I certainly wouldn't have subjected myself to the three-ring circus that CNN called a "town hall," where *my* children were used by the gun control lobby as unwilling tools for a cause they oppose.

At no time did CNN ever correct these smears. And aside from the single Camerota appearance, never did a single producer inquire into such malicious lies. CNN could not bear the thought of allowing a two-sided discussion to jeopardize its narrative. The only person from CNN who considered inviting me on one of its shows was one of Brian Stelter's producers after I Twitter-lectured Stelter regarding his remarks about Sarah Sanders's joining Fox and Sean Spicer's joining *Dancing with the Stars*.[2] The Twitter conversation went like this:

> Stelter: Family ties, Fox style: Sarah Huckabee Sanders joins her father Mike as a Fox contributor. I'm sure we'll see a father-daughter segment at some point. Fox also has a father-son pair in host Steve and reporter Peter Doocy. Wrote this about Spicer and ABC last night, now it applies to Sanders and Fox too: how should ex–White House officials be treated when they spend months misleading the public, then seek positions of fame and privilege?
>
> Me: Disagreement doesn't = willfully misleading. This attitude is partly why people refuse to see others—regardless the party—as anything other than walking issues. It dehumanizes others and the person doing it in the process.

Stelter: We are living through a period of official lying that's unprecedented in our lifetimes. The president misspeaks so much, with such gusto, that it's become the defining feature of his administration. This isn't about "disagreement," as you claimed. It's about deception.

Me: Brian. The previous admin blamed law-abiding people for his gun-running program. He lied about doc access. Clinton folks work with ABC and your network today. To say current time is "unprecedented" is pure partisan hyperbole. People are more than their politics.

I added:

There are those on the left who insist on reducing people to issues because it aids their ability to justify maliciousness. If you want to talk about actual deception, there it is. Seriously— did you all JUST NOW discover a conscience? Sit down.

Stelter's complaint about anyone else's dishonesty when he was too afraid to push back against insane smears on his network of me, my mothering, and my character was too much for me to take silently. Stelter never agreed to have me on. Instead, he interviewed someone in mental health so they could diagnose Trump according to their biases. A big step forward!

Perhaps inspired by all the "child murderer" rhetoric, people began threatening my children and coming to my home. One evening about a month after the Parkland town hall and shortly after we had moved, a friend from our old neighborhood told my husband that someone was trying to get into our old house, which we had not yet put on the market. A member of the local police force, aware of the apparent break-in and realizing that it was our house, called to make sure our family was safe.

We had tried to relocate discreetly to avoid the crazies, but that same week an anti-gun nut in San Francisco doxxed us, posting photos of our new house. My attorney saw it first and called me. I am not a crier, and in the whirlwind that followed the Parkland shooting I had tried to focus on truth, grace, and making the best case I could for law-abiding gun owners. But at that moment I burst into tears. I went into my closet and closed the door so my kids couldn't hear me. The hate that inspired such an inhuman act was overwhelming. The ugliness, the massacre, the grief, the vultures—all of it just broke my heart.

I hadn't felt like this since the early days of the Tea Party. When the opposition turned vicious and I was thinking of giving up, Andrew Breitbart called and screamed at me to continue the fight. "If you back down, why on earth should people with no radio show continue to fight?" he thundered. "It creates a domino effect. We can't do that to people! *You have a responsibility*!"

So once again, with Andrew's words ringing in my mind, I ignored the rage mob and focused on the work at hand. In the weeks and months that followed, I spoke with teachers, families of the Parkland dead, and others whose lives were tragically altered on February 14, 2018. They became friends whose strength is an inspiration to me. Many reached out, some to talk over the phone, others to meet in person. Andy Pollack and his wife visited our home as they road-tripped across the country. I also met young Anthony Borges, the most critically injured of the survivors, and his family. The same age as my oldest son and one of the bravest people I've ever met, Anthony heroically made himself a human shield, blocking the murderer at a classroom door. He gave me a hug when we parted. I wrapped my arms gingerly around his shattered body and prayed for God to take his pain and heal him and his family.

Left-wing would-be journalists who can't get hired anywhere else tend to end up in a dank backwater of the Internet called Media Matters, founded by Clinton ally David Brock and funded by George Soros and the leftist billionaires' club Democracy Alliance. Ironically, at Media Matters *media doesn't matter*. It offers breathless, outraged headlines about how some Fox/Republican/conservative person said something contrary to progressive dogma.

In 2012, in the bloody Helmand province of Afghanistan, a scene of intense fighting, four Marines were videoed urinating on the corpses of Taliban fighters they had just engaged. "These were the same guys that were killing our family, killing our brothers," recalls Sergeant Joseph Chamblin, one of the four Marines. Their gesture of contempt, he says, was psychological warfare.

The reaction was swift. The highest levels of the military condemned the Marines' actions, and commentary from veterans and civilians alike filled cable news. On my radio program, I implored civilians to withhold their judgment, as the military would handle the matter appropriately, and probably more harshly than civilian justice would do. I asked my listeners how they might respond after a brutal fight in which they watched their brother Marines die, adding that I might "drop trou and do it too."

Editing my forty-minute discussion down to two minutes, Media Matters twisted my words to sound as though I advocated urinating on Afghan villagers. Eager to get me fired from CNN, where I was a contributor, it propagated this malicious distortion in story after story. Because hordes of "journalists" too lazy to do their own research use Media Matters as a wire service, simply rewriting its propaganda, the story spread. Without asking for my response or even for the recording of my complete remarks, CNN demanded that I apologize. I refused and said that I would quit first. I would not apologize for Media Matters' distorted version of my words. While I remained friendly with many people at the network, it was best that we parted ways. As for the four Marines, one had all charges against him dismissed; another, suffering from post-traumatic stress syndrome, died of a prescription drug overdose.

I learned that Media Matters assigns a reporter to follow every conservative host or commentator on radio and television. I ran into my own assigned reporter, Joe Strupp, at the airport when I was flying home after CPAC. He informed me that I was his "beat," and we struck up a relationship that, though adversarial, was friendly enough.

The media's favorite target, of course, is President Donald Trump. A study of the press's coverage of his first hundred days in office concluded that 98 percent of media reports were hostile, marking a substantial increase in press antagonism from the previous administration.[3] The Pew Research Center found that the media's coverage of Trump was three times more hostile than their coverage of Obama, only 5 percent of Trump's coverage being positive.[4]

Trump's every breath is depicted as a scandal, but genuine Democratic scandals don't rate a second glance. At the onset of "Impeachmentgate", all the media not in the tank for Elizabeth Warren dutifully ran interference for Joe Biden by insisting that the accusations of corruption against his son Hunter were unsupported by evidence.[5] While Vice President Biden was the Obama administration's main man on Ukrainian policy, Hunter landed a fifty-thousand-dollar-a-month gig with that country's second-largest natural gas producer, Burisma Holdings, despite having absolutely no relevant credentials. We're supposed to accept without question that there is nothing to suggest that the VP exerted his influence to have the investigator in a Burisma Holdings corruption probe tossed. We're not supposed to think it's fishy that the VP was the U.S. point man on Ukraine while his son occupied a lucrative sinecure at one of its major companies? The Obama administration was apparently worried about a conflict, because it was vetting the younger Biden until Joe reacted angrily.[6]

This isn't the first or tenth time that legacy media have abandoned their duties while insisting that questioning their ethics is somehow dangerous to a "free" press. During Trump's first term, the media focused almost exclusively on controversies that they tried unsuccessfully to make into impeachable offenses.[7] Many of the administration's initial accomplishments—deregulation, protecting religious freedom, improving veterans' care, transforming the courts, and increasing energy production—went underreported, if they were reported at all.[8] Instead, airtime went to stories like these:

1. Slate, along with the *Washington Post*, insisted that Trump had set up a secret server through which he could surreptitiously communicate with Russia, a story that later other outlets were forced to debunk.[9]

2. The *Washington Post* falsely accused the Trump administration of denying passports to Latinos.[10]

3. CNN falsely reported that Republicans had funded the infamous Trump-Russia dossier concocted by the opposition research firm Fusion GPS.[11]

4. Media reported that an advisor to Ukraine's president, Volodymyr Zelensky, knew firsthand that Trump had demanded that Zelensky investigate Hunter Biden if he wanted to speak with or otherwise meet him. Outlets that reported the falsehood were forced to retract their stories.

5. CNN,[12] MSNBC, CBS,[13] and other outlets reported that the Trump campaign colluded with Russian-linked hackers to obtain WikiLeaks emails. The email on which the story rested turned out to have been sent after the WikiLeaks documents had already been made public.

6. ABC's Brian Ross reported that Trump ordered his national security advisor, General Michael Flynn, to contact the Russians during the 2016 election. Ross failed to report that the request was made *after* the election, at which point it is common for incoming administrations to establish relations with foreign governments. ABC modified its story (which was entirely predicated on this false premise, so a clarification wasn't helpful) and barred Ross from covering Trump.[14]

7. When Trump asserted that Russia paid the Clintons millions of dollars in connection with the infamous Uranium One deal, the media, led by *Newsweek*, reported that the

charge was false.[15] It was true, as none other than the *New York Times* acknowledged:

As the Russians gradually assumed control of Uranium One in three separate transactions from 2009 to 2013, Canadian records show, a flow of cash made its way to the Clinton Foundation. Uranium One's chairman used his family foundation to make four donations totaling $2.35 million. Those contributions were not publicly disclosed by the Clintons, despite an agreement Mrs. Clinton had struck with the Obama White House to publicly identify all donors. Other people with ties to the company made donations as well.

And shortly after the Russians announced their intention to acquire a majority stake in Uranium One, Mr. Clinton received $500,000 for a Moscow speech from a Russian investment bank with links to the Kremlin that was promoting Uranium One stock.[16]

Americans remain largely distrustful of media, their level of approval having dropped four percentage points to 41 percent from 2018 to 2019.[17] Trump isn't just battling Democrats; he's battling the legacy press, which becomes outraged every time he exposes its "fake news."

In 2007, a left-leaning journalist set up a Google Groups forum, known as JournoList, for four hundred other left-leaning journalists, many of them quite prominent. Conservative journalists were banned. Within these comfortable confines, the members discussed how to kill the stories about Obama's radical hometown pastor, Jeremiah Wright,[18] why the federal government should shut down Fox News,[19] how to tar Tea Partiers as "Nazis,"[20] and how to brand those who challenge their narratives as "racists."[21] It was all good fun until *Politico* reported on the group. The Daily Caller and the *Wall Street Journal* followed up on the story, and it quickly became notorious.

Conservatives' darkest suspicions of a left-wing journalistic conspiracy having been confirmed, the left was outraged when the right began acting as if there were a left-wing journalistic conspiracy. "Trump Allies Target Journalists Over Coverage Deemed Hostile to White House," screamed a *New York Times* headline in August 2019. Kenneth Vogel breathlessly reported that a "loose network of conservative operatives allied with the White House is pursuing what they say will be an aggressive operation to discredit news organizations deemed hostile to President Trump by publicizing damaging information about journalists...."[22]

A. G. Sulzberger, the newspaper's publisher, weighed in, declaring, "The goal of this campaign is clearly to intimidate journalists from doing their job, which includes serving as a check on power and exposing wrongdoing when it occurs. The *Times* will not be intimidated or silenced."

If the "Milkshake Duck" chapter proved anything, it's that the media have long favored intimidating American citizens by shaming them for their beliefs. It's easier than debating the issues. But they were apoplectic when someone used this same tactic on *them*. CNN, a notorious doxxer, has its own "reporter" who scours conservatives' Twitter, Instagram, and Facebook feeds.[23] The network tracked down a guy on Reddit who made a GIF of President Trump body-slamming a wrestler with the CNN logo superimposed on his face and threatened to doxx him for it.[24] That the network treated this like serious journalism is a marvel. Having terrified its target, CNN smugly reported its victory: "Now the user is apologizing, writing in a lengthy post on Reddit that he does not advocate violence against the press and expressing remorse there and in an interview with CNN for other posts he made that were racist and anti-Semitic."

In his cringing retraction, the man wrote, "The meme was created purely as satire, it was not meant to be a call to violence against CNN or any other news affiliation," as if that weren't obvious. Having achieved

its goal of humiliating a nonconformist, CNN dismissed him with a
supercilious kick to the backside as he crouched in abasement:

> CNN is not publishing [the man's] name because he is a pri-
> vate citizen who has issued an extensive statement of apology,
> showed his remorse by saying he has taken down all his
> offending posts, and because he said he is not going to repeat
> this ugly behavior on social media again. In addition, he said
> his statement could serve as an example to others not to do
> the same.
>
> CNN reserves the right to publish his identity should any
> of that change.

Good grief—if that isn't a threat, then what is? CNN: The Nanny
of the Internet. Numerous other "journalists" applauded CNN for the
important job of taking to task the highly newsworthy anonymous Redditor and his nation-endangering wrestling GIFs.

This all reminds me of my favorite paragraph from that aforementioned *New York Times* article: "But using journalistic techniques to
target journalists and news organizations as retribution for—or as a
warning not to pursue—coverage critical of the president is fundamen-
tally different from the well-established role of the news media in scru-
tinizing people in positions of power."

Yes, people in positions of "power," like this anonymous, GIF-
posting Redditor. Or the elderly woman CNN ambushed at her house
after it discovered that she ran a Facebook page for Trump supporters
that unknowingly promoted a Russian-coordinated event. The network
blasted her full name on the airwaves and showed her house number in
its footage; she says she received threats as a result.[25] Or the black day
laborer whom the Daily Beast gleefully doxxed because he administered
a Facebook group on which a facetiously doctored video of Nancy Pelosi
was shared. Having tracked down the man believed responsible for this

forbidden expression of disrespect, the Daily Beast trumpeted every unhappy detail of the man's life to the public.[26]

The media expend more effort censuring people who criticize them or their preferred politicians than they do on stories like Fast and Furious, Benghazi, or illegal immigration.

After the Parkland town hall, those "journalists" who were unfamiliar with my radio program or history in media began a deep dive into my social media history hoping to find something offensive to use as a means of discrediting the policies I supported. *Newsweek* published two articles informing the public that I have, over the past ten years, published a handful of tweets proclaiming my dislike of Neil Young's music. Yes, the intrepid investigative journalists of *Newsweek* had dug through ten years of my Twitter archives and come out with a fistful of Neil Young tweets.

"[Former] NRA SPOKESWOMAN DANA LOESCH HAS BEEN RAILING AGAINST NEIL YOUNG FOR MORE THAN 20 YEARS," blared the headline.[27] (Confession: This has been the desktop wallpaper on my computer since the story was published.) I was more perplexed by the fact that Twitter had been around that long than by the seriousness that *Newsweek* attributed to my tweets. Not to be outdone in the bizarre journalizing department, the Daily Beast dramatically published this stunning news under a red seventy-point headline: "Neil Young Fires Back at His Biggest Troll, Dana Loesch: 'I'm Glad I Got Under Her Skin.'"[28]

I'm going to go out on a limb here and suggest that of all the people in the world, I am not Young's "biggest" critic—what they now call a "troll." (Aristotle once said of trolling: "Criticism is something we can avoid easily by saying nothing, doing nothing, and being nothing.") Somewhere out there is a sad person who has toiled in obscurity scribbling denunciations of Young's work, angry that his life's mission was hijacked by the media who tried to make some mom from Dallas out to be Young's biggest enemy.

Numerous other outlets jumped on the story—The Onion's A.V. Club, Pitchfork, Paste, *Spin*—there was so much interest that I was tempted to make Neil Young criticism a full-time gig! The Daily Beast published a story by a humorless sad sack who tracked down Young at the South by Southwest festival in Austin. After she breathlessly read him my tweets, he replied, "'Why doesn't she just shoot me?' before quickly correcting himself: 'You know, I hate to say that because I have kids, and I really don't want anybody to shoot me. I've still got to bring up my kids, so don't take that seriously!'"

The partisan hysteria of the media is not journalism but hackery, designed to stoke division. They manufactured outrage when *Terminator: 6* was released and with the casting announcement for the live-action *Little Mermaid*.[29] Their obsessions are beyond parody. The sad truth is that Americans have lost their respect for and trust in the press, and for good reason. The media denounce President Trump as a would-be dictator when he dismisses them as purveyors of "fake news," but he is simply expressing the views of the people themselves, who realize they cannot rely on the self-important, self-appointed guardians of democracy.

CHAPTER EIGHT

A Time for Anger

"Anger's the anesthetic of the mind."

—C. S. Lewis

Sometimes anger is the only appropriate response.

Sometimes you have every right to be angry. Sometimes, just sometimes, you need to be angry.

Sometimes the offense is so great that only outrage will do. Outrage, a commodity that should be treated as both radioactive and precious, should be reserved for only the most serious of offenses. There have been times in our nation's history when fury and violence were justified. The abolition of slavery, for instance, was worth fighting for. In World War II, the Allies endured horrible suffering to stop even more horrible evils. But violence should be the rare exception, not the primary playbook.

Today, however, outrage is just another political tactic.

In the fall of 2019, the Speaker of the House, Nancy Pelosi, allowed proceedings for the impeachment of President Trump to go forward. The impeachment was not a response to "high crimes and misdemeanors" uncovered by a legitimate investigation but an act of political rage. It was the result of a calculation by the Democrats of how angry they could make the public. We've reverted to the evidentiary standards of the Salem witch trials.

What the left did to Brett Kavanaugh *was* worthy of outrage. Accused of rape, branded "evil,"[1] and called a threat to "the lives of millions of Americans for decades to come,"[2] Kavanaugh was then denounced for appearing angry. The destruction of his reputation, insisted the Democrats, was deserved. *Take your beatings.* One of the brashest formulations of this "argument" is found in a single paragraph by Eliot Cohen in *The Atlantic*:

> Perhaps the collapse of modern conservatism came out most clearly in Kavanaugh's own testimony—its self-pity, its hysteria, its conjuring up of conspiracies, its vindictiveness. He and his family had no doubt suffered agonies. But if we expect steely resolve from a police officer confronting a knife-wielding assailant, or disciplined courage from a firefighter rushing into a burning house, we should expect stoic self-control and calm from a conservative judge, even if his heart is being eaten out. No one watching those proceedings could imagine that a Democrat standing before this judge's bench in the future would get a fair hearing. This was not the conservative temperament on display. It was, rather, personalized grievance politics.[3]

I'm sorry, but circumstances require me to be frank: Is Cohen on meth?

David French, writing at *National Review*, offered a different perspective on Kavanaugh's indignation:

> This was the moment when a member of the "establishment," the person who is supposed to sit quietly, respond mildly, and understand the pain of their opponents without voicing their own anguish, to absorb anger without showing anger, finally said "enough." And he did so with great passion in his own defense, and no rancor against Christine Blasey Ford....

Kavanaugh's indignation resonated with me, as it did with so many other wives, mothers, aunts, grandmothers, and friends. French beautifully noted:

> ... Kavanaugh has been subjected to a series of abhorrent, unsubstantiated allegations culminating in a fantastical and grotesque allegation of gang rape that all too many Serious People took all too seriously. In these circumstances, there was a need—a crying need—for a person to echo the immortal words, "Have you no decency, sir? At long last, have you left no sense of decency." Today, was that moment. Today, there were conservatives across the nation who choked up— some openly wept—during his testimony. Not because they disrespect women. Not because they excuse sexual assault. But because they also love their sons. Because they are tired of being painted as evil when they are seeking to do what's right. Because they want to see a man fight with honor.
>
> That's what Brett Kavanaugh did today. He fought with passion, evidence, and compassion.

My God, I will not abandon a good man who fights with honor, and the day our country does is the day virtue is dead.

Some have insisted that Kavanaugh should not have displayed any emotion at all. Charlie Sykes, for instance, sets an interesting standard:

> The problem was not that Judge Kavanaugh was angry; it was the way he chose to vent his anger. There are appropriate and inappropriate ways of expressing anger, even in the Age of Trump. Prudence and restraint are good ideas for all of us in our daily life, but are essential qualities for a jurist. It is one thing for Lindsey Graham to audition for the role of the Senate's angry Uriah Heep. It is quite another for a Supreme Court nominee to go Full Trump.

To be sure, Trumpism has shattered the norms of politics and civility, but last week we saw the blast zone extended to the judiciary.[4]

Apparently, the accusations of gang rape and drugging women were all Trump's fault! Trump! The Bad Orange Man rigged the entire thing to encourage voter enthusiasm, raise his own approval, and get another toady on the Supreme Court! I've heard of 3D political chess before, but this is on an entirely new level, which, if I'm being honest, impresses me.

Kavanaugh had every right to be angry and to defend himself with the burning passion of a thousand suns. I would have lost respect for him had he not defended himself as strongly as he did. If ever there was a time to raise one's voice, *this was it*. If Kavanaugh had brandished a shoe at the Judiciary Committee like *la chancla*, then okay, maybe there'd be an argument about optics. But Kavanaugh expressed a *righteous anger* at the disparaging of his character. And it wasn't only Kavanaugh who suffered the pain of these attacks—his wife, daughters, parents, and friends all felt the sting of the defamation indulged by Senate Democrats and the press. These are smears that will follow him for life

Refusal to fight such smears emboldens those who make them. Someone who is smeared has not only the right but the *obligation* to knock these smear merchants back on their heels. There is a difference between righteous indignation, petulant whining, and the outrage exhibited by bloodthirsty mobs. I feel my friend Charlie Sykes misses this obvious point.

Righteous anger is justified, defensible, definable, and limited because it is purposeful and dissipates. Outrage is unbridled, contagious, impossible to control, and often undefinable. And as we've seen from countless examples, it serves no purpose but to glorify those who express it.

The media were horrified when they discovered that their long-standing practice of unearthing old comments from social media to excoriate someone, defining him by his silliest, most awkward, or most awful moment, was going to be turned against them. The *New York Times* reported:

> A loose network of conservative operatives allied with the White House is pursuing what they say will be an aggressive operation to discredit news organizations deemed hostile to President Trump by publicizing damaging information about journalists.
>
> It is the latest step in a long-running effort by Mr. Trump and his allies to undercut the influence of legitimate news reporting. Four people familiar with the operation described how it works, asserting that it has compiled dossiers of potentially embarrassing social media posts and other public statements by hundreds of people who work at some of the country's most prominent news organizations....
>
> Operatives have closely examined more than a decade's worth of public posts and statements by journalists.... Only a fraction of what the network claims to have uncovered has been made public, the people said, with more to be disclosed as the 2020 election heats up.[5]

The Daily Caller collected some of the hand-wringing reactions. The *Times*' publisher, A. G. Sulzberger, fretted, "This represents an escalation of an ongoing campaign against the free press. For years the president has used terms like 'fake news' and 'enemy of the people' to demonize journalists and journalism." Joy Reid of MSNBC tweeted, "Welcome to the age of digital brownshirtism." But Seth Mandel of the *Washington Examiner* was unimpressed: "If you're a conservative journalist, you have been the target of this behavior by leftist 'think tanks'—which are the same ones spoon-feeding reporters their scoops. So what these reporters are calling a 'war on the press' is an admission they've been waging this war for years."[6]

The greatest threat to the integrity and freedom of journalism comes from journalists themselves, too many of whom are ideological hacks practicing the journalism of destruction—doxxing private persons, omitting or fabricating information, presenting opinion as fact. These people do not represent a "free" press. They're a *servile* press—servile to a blinding ideology that commands their total obedience.

Righteous indignation is different from the "rage" of the 1960s radicals and today's social justice warriors. If the latter kind of anger is not properly contained and managed, it burns up everything in its vicinity. Because it requires constant rekindling with the discovery of new outrage, there are only two options: let it die or feed it, knowing that every time you give it fuel you risk losing control of it.

If someone is angry, it is because someone made him that way. Political disagreements are viewed as personal slights, and the resulting response is anger. Anger is viewed as toughness, regardless of the context. How angry you are indicates how correct you are. Being loud helps, too. Every politician delivers the same angry applause lines, the same angry platitudes. They're thought-killers. Wooing voters in this way shouldn't inspire confidence in anyone's ability to make law.

Politics has always made some people angry, but now *everyone* is angry. As a result, anger is less fun and less likely to attract notice unless you ramp it up to outrage or fury. The extreme political tribalism of our time acknowledges only two truths: Our way is the right way, and their way is the wrong way. Caution is for the weak, as is fact-checking.

Just as shock is the laziest form of art, anger is the laziest form of political analysis and participation.

I've heard people on both the right and the left classify anger as a tactic. It is impossible to overlook the righteous indignation that turned voters away from the party that would sooner classify them as racists and deplorables than as Americans who chose Trump for good reasons. Progressives and socialists responded to that righteous indignation with fury and more fury. Non-progressives and non-socialists responded to *their* fury with anger of their own. Everyone thinks his anger is righteous because he believes his cause, and his cause alone, is just.

"My dear brothers and sisters, take note of this: Everyone should be quick to speak and slow to become angry, because human anger does not produce the righteousness that God desires." (James 1:19–20)

I'm not sure when it began, but over the past several years I have made an effort to tame my tongue. I've done this because I have felt guilty about not always using the incredible platform God has given me in a way that honors Him and reflects His purpose. No one and nothing else matters. You can't say you're fighting on God's behalf while using the devil's tactics. It's a poor ambassador for liberty and grace who is constantly furious and loud. How can we purport to be a loving and inclusive people if anger is our only mode? How can we purport to be the people of reason and logic if we allow ourselves to be overruled by our passions? I'm not saying that anger is never the proper response, but anger has been *the* response for so long that it has become commonplace. Outrage, a reaction previously reserved for the most heinous of acts, is now an everyday feeling because anger has become ordinary.

Some, particularly those who don't believe in redemption, might find this a little hard to take coming from me. That it is *coming from me* should be a warning sign. When *people like me* tell you it's gone too far, the hair on your arm should stand at attention. When *people like me* realize that things need to change, beginning from within, *you should listen.* It's like Colonel Sanders saying, "You know, perhaps I've fried too much chicken."

Others will think I'm surrendering. You're right—in a way I am. I'm surrendering this ridiculous outrage tactic to God. I will never bend a knee to the rage mob, but I gratefully bend a knee to God daily. If you haven't surrendered your plan to God, you've surrendered to yourself, an infinitely less capable master.

I'm not trying to change others. I'm not perfect. I struggle daily. In fact, I struggled with myself through every page of this book. I'm changing myself, and if others believe the cause of the country is as important as they say it is, they will do the same. They will change from within and learn to listen and discuss instead of rage and cancel.

Nevertheless, we have always had political strife in this country. Democratic congressman Preston Brooks beat Republican senator Charles Sumner nearly to death with a cane in the Senate chamber. Aaron Burr, while he was still vice president of the United States, killed Alexander Hamilton in a duel. Thomas Jefferson once referred to the ascendancy of federalist rule as the "reign of witches."[7] We will never achieve perfect decorum in our politics, but I think we have matured somewhat in resolving disagreements. There will always be political factions, but the most prosperous and fruitful times in our nation's history have come when factions are balanced and dialogue is possible. Unfortunately, we've been using the extremists among us as get-out-the-vote agents and allowing them to direct the national dialogue.

People have been poked, pushed, libeled, slandered, smeared, and impugned for so long that they have finally snapped. And if we're being honest, that was the goal all along. If this is the new normal, how do you manage it? And how do Christians wage the culture war and advance their values without joining in the ugliness?

The truth is it *will* get ugly. Christians should know this. Scripture says—and I'm paraphrasing here—"It's super yuck out there, so ask the Holy Spirit to give you restraint and words."

The left has "resist;" we have "restraint." We must restrain our worst emotions and challenge ourselves to respond in love as we put what we have learned to the test. It's not easy, but Christians can't simply check out. Either you're here in the world to win souls and soften hearts or you just want to stay in your hobbit hole (and bury your talents), sinning as little as possible until Jesus comes back.

Conservatives have always been the nice ones, the accommodating political class, the group no one was genuinely worried about offending because they never responded in any other manner beyond praying for you. Maybe they wouldn't bring you a casserole if your grandma died. There were no protests, no boycotts. No one was worried that someone would cut off his head if he insulted Jesus. And then, after a couple generations' worth of denigration, conservatives *exploded*.

I can't say that I blame them.

The Tea Party movement was as much a reaction against the Republican establishment as it was to the Democrats.

The fear is that good Americans will be so frustrated at having been abused by politicians and the media that their hearts will be primed for a tyrant—an actual tyrant, not simply someone the left dislikes because his political ideology opposes their own.

No one should have to deal with character assassination or with the threat of being doxxed simply for speaking his mind on social media. Believe me, I know how infuriating it is. Let me warn you though: The right is forgetting how to be happy warriors. Let me help. Here are three golden rules:

1. *You don't have to attend every fight you're invited to.*

Pick your battles. Sometimes a fight is worth it if you disrupt a narrative, correct a falsehood, or defend someone's honor. But don't kid yourself that every fight is *the* fight and that truth, justice, and the American way depend on your responding in kind to every knucklehead's tweet. Over the past decade, I have watched plenty of people go from happy activists to miserable, rage-filled polemicists. Many of them go too hard and suffer burnout. Some have the untamed zealotry of a new convert, which isn't bad, but can burn out an activist quickly.

Some days I wake up, check the news cycle, roll my eyes, and beg the Holy Spirit to put his hand over my mouth. I've seen *Jerry Springer* episodes with more class and decency than some of our recent news cycles. For crying out loud, CNN put a white supremacist on TV and titled him as such in the lower third, just to take a jab at the administration. I was half expecting the network to introduce the dude as its special White Nationalist correspondent, and I say that only half facetiously.

2. *Be a happy warrior.*

Anything worth fighting for is worth fighting for with a good spirit and lots of heart. There is no reason to make yourself miserable with a bad attitude. Don't be like the left in assuming the ill will of everyone you meet. This is the lack of grace that is rotting our national discourse, our political system, and even our culture.

3. *Let your first motivation be love, not ambition.*

A huge part of politics is a competition to see who is the most ruthless because ruthlessness is a virtue only in politics.

A friend once remarked, "You don't win a war by standing on moral high ground." To that I say, if you can't win a war by occupying the moral high ground, you're fighting the wrong war. How do we fight to restore virtue by fighting without virtue? Are we to believe that morality, ethics, and virtue are now weaknesses? Limitations? Liabilities? What good is victory if we become the very thing we're fighting? Is that not the definition of defeat? These notions are not coming from godless, weak, or unengaged people. These are good, hardworking people, some of whom I know and respect—people who love their families and their country, people pushed to their limits.

That, friends, is the point: *They are pushed to their limits*, and with patience spent, they feel justified in getting into the mud with people who refuse to dwell anywhere else. You will never out-bad people who have spent a lifetime perfecting badness. You who work at living in the light will never outperform those who insist on living in darkness.

We can't win over hearts and minds by hardening them further. Here is the truth: Some people will never be convinced—ever. There is nothing you can do, nothing you can say that will overcome their pride, their ego, and their vanity. They aren't worth your effort. The people who are worth your effort are those whose minds aren't completely shut. People are convinced not by our flexing but by our thoughtful arguments based in stewardship.

Please don't mistake me: I'm not made of kittens and sunshine. I'm not suggesting that anyone compromise his beliefs or fight the good fight only with bake sales and offers of free hugs. In fact, I'm suggesting the opposite: Grow stronger in your stance, firmer in your arguments, but save your outrage for the truly outrageous.

"My dear brothers and sisters, take note of this: Everyone should be quick to listen, slow to speak, and slow to become angry, because human anger does not produce the righteousness that God desires." (James 1:19–20)

After the righteous indignation, when the dust settles, there must be a righteous reconciliation.

Sometimes the victory is simply recognizing that others think differently. Sometimes you just have to give it to God and continue being a happy warrior for your own cause. This doesn't mean there isn't space for reconciliation. To the contrary, amiable relations depends upon grace, and grace is in short supply.

CHAPTER NINE

Make Grace Great Again

*"Jesus Ratioed On Twitter for Saying
'Love Your Enemies'"*

—*Babylon Bee*

This is how partisan we've become: David Platt, pastor of McLean Bible Church in suburban Washington, apologized to his congregation for praying over a sinner who had showed up at his church. The sinner in question was President Donald Trump, whose motorcade had made an unscheduled stop in Northern Virginia, en route back to the White House, to pray for the victims of a mass shooting in Virginia Beach that had claimed twelve innocent lives.

"Sometimes we find ourselves in situations that we didn't see coming," Platt said in his semi-apology.[1] "[W]e're faced with a decision in a moment when we don't have the liberty of deliberation, so we do our best to glorify God." Platt defended his actions further in a letter to his parishioners on the church's website, writing, "Based on this text, I know that it is good, and pleasing in the sight of God, to pray for the president. So in that moment, I decided to take this unique opportunity for us as a church to pray over him together. My aim was in no way to endorse the president, his policies, or his party, but to obey God's command to pray for our president and other leaders to govern in the way this passage portrays."[2]

Platt said that after he received the unexpected request from President Trump for prayers, he had thought of the exhortation in 1 Timothy 2:1–6 to pray for political leaders: "I urge, then, first of all, that petitions, prayers, intercession, and thanksgiving be made for all people—for kings and all those in authority, that we may live peaceful and quiet lives in all godliness and holiness. This is good, and pleases God our Savior, who wants all people to be saved and to come to a knowledge of the truth. For there is one God and one mediator between God and mankind, the man Christ Jesus, who gave himself as a ransom for all people. This has now been witnessed to at the proper time."[3]

Platt wrote, "[W]hile I am thankful that we had an opportunity to obey 1 Timothy 2 in a unique way today, I don't want to purposely ever do anything that undermines the unity we have in Christ." His letter was immediately politicized by political factions on the right. It was alleged that he had apologized simply for praying, which he clearly did not do. Why should he have? He had acknowledged those in his congregation who were offended and stressed the importance of Christian unity.

It isn't David Platt who is turning Trump into an obstacle to faith, but the many Jonahs sitting in the pews of McLean Bible Church. Did his disaffected congregants think that Trump was beyond redemption, beyond prayer? Did they forget that the shepherd will leave his flock of ninety-nine sheep to look for the one lost? Did they forget that God will meet them where they are, always? Did they forget their responsibilities as sons and daughters of God? Have they forgotten just how much God loves? That faith is inclusive? Have they forgotten the boundless purpose of grace?

There has been a fight between two factions of the right regarding faith and Trump. It goes something like this: One faction believes that support for Trump's presidency amounts to an endorsement of all his previous bad behavior. It's an argument that would make the Pharisees proud. It's impossible to separate the good policy Trump has proposed from the sins of which he's accused. If you're *really* a Christian, some in this faction assert, you'll condemn him wholly and outright. Trump, they say, is unfit for office because he is morally compromised. He's bossy and loud, they say, even on Twitter. He mocks women's appearances, criticizes dead veterans, and considers entertaining every petty fracas he encounters. He's a sinner! True, and yet it doesn't disqualify him from office.

The other faction believes that Trump, like all mankind, is a sinner but that God has a purpose for everyone. Some preachers and pastors in this group have appeared on various cable news networks as character witnesses of sorts for either Trump or Christian voters, and more than a few have suggested that Trump is in the White House because God put him there and can use him. The wing of the right that claims that you can't be both a Christian and a Trump supporter scoff at these assertions and accuse these evangelicals of compromising their faith for power. It's a specious claim that misunderstands not only what these Christian leaders have stated, but also the omnipotence of God in the Bible. Their premise is that God can't use Trump because he is flawed. This contradicts biblical teaching—the most flawed people in the Bible were called by God into his service for his glory, and he alone will raise up and equip those he calls for these tasks. God called David and Judah, both sinners. Jesus himself came from a line of some of the most corrupt and sinful men in biblical history. Saul of Tarsus, a brutal man who hunted down and murdered Christians in an attempt to exterminate the faith, was called to conversion on the road to Damascus. Saul, whose reputation as "the wolf who stalked the lambs" preceded him around the known world, became Paul, the apostle to the Gentiles and one of the most important Christian figures in the post-apostolic period. To argue that sinful people cannot serve God's purpose is to deny the omnipotence of God. As my pastor once said, "God doesn't call the equipped, He equips the called."

I didn't always feel this way. Until just a couple of years ago I wasn't always fighting with myself to focus on grace instead of punishment. As I write this, my name is trending nationwide on Twitter in conjunction with the shuttering of NRATV due to an ongoing fight between the NRA and its longtime PR firm, Ackerman McQueen. Remarks such as "Get shot and burn in hell," "Go suck your gun barrel," and the like make up the tenor of the rude and lewd comments. My initial response is not one of grace. My initial response is one of utter fury and righteous indignation, rage at those small people who would imperil long–fought for Second Amendment rights with power jockeying and shortsighted pettiness. Grace takes effort. It is not even my second or third response. I have to actively choose it, and the choice is a struggle.

I'm sometimes mad that choosing grace over hate is something I *should* do. I'm also angry with myself for not displaying grace more often. I have found that the times when I least felt like it were the times grace was needed the most. I'm so often Jonah, fleeing the call of Christian duty. Choosing grace and finding mercy for those who seem undeserving is my Nineveh. I'm tempted to believe that wretched people like the Twitter trolls I referenced above don't deserve the energy and strength it takes *not* to strike back. I'm tempted to destroy instead of persuade, not because I can't make a persuasive, substantive argument, but because I don't care to. Just like Jonah, I judged those people as unworthy of hearing the truth or benefiting from my effort to present an opposing argument. Cruelty is quicker and more satisfying. Our clickbait culture proves it.

To remind myself to try to see people as people and not as walking issues, eight years ago I had Ephesians 6:12–13 tattooed on my right forearm:

For our struggle is not against flesh and blood, but against the rulers, against the authorities, against the powers of this dark world and against the spiritual forces of evil in the heavenly realms. Therefore put on the full armor of God, so that when the day of evil comes, you may be able to stand your ground, and after you have done everything, to stand.

I've used my tattoo to witness to celebrities and political figures who never would have read scripture had it not been there on my forearm for them to see at an event or in a greenroom. It also serves as a daily reminder for myself. The only reason I or any of us is saved is solely because Jesus doesn't look on us like Jonah looked on Nineveh. Jesus meets us where we are.

When I first began in politics eleven or so years ago, I was all fire and brimstone. I had the zeal of a new convert, though I had fully embraced conservatism some seven years earlier.

It was the early days of the Tea Party, a movement I played a part in founding and organizing. The movement exploded in a week, in part due to conservatives' early dominance on social media platforms. We fought being yoked with government's bad decisions. The sudden realization that the country was at a crossroads both politically and culturally was jarring because we had been apathetic, preferring to protest in the pages of the *Wall Street Journal* and by talking politics in the parking lot after church.

On my Sunday night radio show, I helped organize the first Tea Party in my hometown of St. Louis. I used my growing platform to attract motivated, like-minded people, which helped the movement to grow. The first rally took place on a cold, sunny day under the St. Louis Arch, on the riverfront. It was the first time I had ever seen so many people who thought like me assemble in one place at the same time. They had come from all over the state. Some had awoken before dawn and driven for hours. They'd brought their American flags, their Gadsden flags, white-boards, and Sharpies. They'd brought their kids, their friends, their parents. What we hadn't brought was a sound system, but I had a tiny bullhorn in my car, something I used now and then as a joke on air. I kicked off the rally with that tiny bullhorn; several years later conservatives from across the country rallied again in the same spot, with massive screens and musical artists who gave up their time to fly in and perform on a huge stage.

In those days my tone was one of fiery indignation. I eschewed podiums and ran around the stage with the mic. Twice I jumped off the stage after a speech to confront critics and hecklers face to face. (In my mind I'm six foot eight and pushing three hundred pounds; in reality I'm five foot six and one hundred thirty-five pounds—quite the difference.) I went to Wisconsin, where rioters damaged the state capitol and tried to take down Governor Scott Walker during two recalls (they finally got him in 2016). Wisconsin was also the place where a partisan prosecutor conducted predawn raids on Walker volunteers' homes, pulling children out of their beds and assembling terrified families on their lawns in front of blinding searchlights while a tipped-off reporter snapped a picture for the papers.[4]

As I was closing my remarks there at a rally for then Lieutenant Governor Rebecca Kleefisch, some of the union protesters in the back began yelling at me. I thanked the crowd, jumped off the stage, and made a beeline for the largest and loudest man in the group, clad in overalls. I demanded to know why he had a problem with any of the rally-goers, specifically me. He seemed surprised at my forthrightness and went on about my being a "Koch whore." (A repeated progressive refrain of the early Tea Party era was that we conservatives only cared about people's rights because we were paid to do so by the Koch brothers' Americans for Prosperity, though I never saw a check.) I told him that his hostility took me by surprise, since most hardworking, blue-collar folks in my experience were gracious people, while his manners were shocking. He was taken aback and calmed down. We then proceeded to have an illuminating discussion about wages, immigration, and contracts with the community in the context of public sector unions. While we still didn't agree on everything at the conversation's end, no one was yelling at anyone anymore. We thanked each other for the discussion, and I left bearing him no ill will.

My oldest son provoked a change within me a couple of years ago, a turning to grace. A week after the Parkland shooting, he and his brother were mentioned onstage at one of CNN's town halls as political ammunition. They angrily denounced being used in such a way. "That kid does not speak for me," my oldest told me angrily, speaking of the teen a year or so older than he who mentioned him and his brother. "Keep any reference to my mother and my brother out of your mouth."

This incident sparked my son's political awakening. He began participating in debate, following some of the bigger news stories and making himself familiar with firearm laws. He expressed an interest in attending law school to study constitutional law, so he could someday defend our natural and civil rights. It was by watching his reaction to the hate I regularly received that I realized I needed to model an overabundance of grace in order to offset that hatred. I needed to model for him how not to let the world harden your heart. Just as becoming a mother forged me as a conservative, watching my oldest son become more politically inclined has impressed upon me the importance of demonstrating grace, particularly in the absence of it.

Unfortunately, as you have learned, outrage is an industry. Organizations like Media Matters and Raw Story exist to manufacture it, and other groups such as the Southern Poverty Law Center and Everytown seek to keep divisions deep. Promoting strife is profitable, and some are not willing to give up the paycheck. Thus, those who disagree on certain issues are "racists," those who would rather not give up their Second Amendment rights are "murderers," and black Americans who disagree with the Democratic Party platform are abused and slandered, as are women who disagree with taxpayer-funded abortion on demand.

As I have said, I wasn't always inclined towards grace. Just as becoming a mother forged me into a conservative, so too, has motherhood taught me to embrace grace. Some days are harder than others. But the effort must be made; my two young sons are watching me from backstage, off camera, on TV, listening on the radio, reading my words on social media. If the only example I ever set for them is that of outrage, that is all they will learn. Parenting is a sacrifice of ego—and so is genuine discussion of varied ideas. I realized this all the more the day we moved my oldest son into his freshman dorm. My self-soothing techniques are superfluous organization and tidying, so I was in charge of helping him pack. The weeks leading up to his departure felt like palliative care for the end of his childhood. I was so prepared in every way: storage boxes, clothing bags, rolling plastic drawers, twin XL bedding, supplies, etc. I wasn't prepared for what it *felt like*. I think part of our fear as we release our children into the world stems from wondering if we've adequately prepared them to live in an unkind world without its breaking their spirit and making them unkind as well.

I first had to realize that grace and justice are not mutually exclusive, and they can coexist. In fact, they must coexist. Civil society relies on civility in the face of incivility, else incivility becomes the norm when the goal should be to make *civility* the norm. I like the idea of living in such a way that others question their choices, not as a form of punishment, but as reconciliation. The sting of selfishness is never very far away, and the temptation to indulge in mean-spirited replies can be very strong. The effort it takes to curtail one's tongue is exhausting.

In this era of hyper-partisanship, where lines are even drawn on a church sanctuary's floor, we need grace, forgiveness, and reconciliation in politics more than ever. I am drawn to what I interpret to be Jesus's humor in Mark 3:17, when he refers to James and his brother John as "sons of thunder." By all accounts, in the beginning James and John were brawlers, rough men, young in faith and rich in zeal. They were no-nonsense and—as demonstrated by a couple of incidents in the Bible— short on grace and mercy. In Luke 9:49–50 John tells Jesus, "Master, we saw someone driving out demons in your name and we tried to stop him, because he is not one of us." Jesus corrects him and says, "Do not stop him, for whoever is not against you is for you." It's a strategy I've often heard wisely repeated in various forms within Republican politics, but one I've not seen followed lately. In the past, I have been guilty of not following it myself. Reagan's "Your 80-percent friend is not your 20-per-cent enemy" echoes this wisdom in a way. Republicans and conservatives spend as much time tearing each other down as Democrats do building each other up.

Later in Luke 9, as Jesus travels to Jerusalem, he sends messengers ahead of him to a Samaritan village. But the villagers will have none of it, because Jesus is heading to Jerusalem first. When James and John see this, Luke 9:54 says that the "sons of thunder" asked Jesus, "Lord, do you want us to call fire down from heaven to destroy them?" Jesus rebukes them, and they all travel to another village. These two headstrong disciples didn't stay that way; they were changed by their mission. James was the first of the twelve disciples to be martyred, and John was later known as the Apostle of Love. They were changed by God and learned that their mission to persuade hearts and minds and save souls was bigger than any power they were later granted authority to use. They were prepared for the bigger responsibility that awaited them later in life.

If the men whom Jesus called the sons of thunder could change, then surely we can also. James and John were certainly not weakened by their shift toward grace, but rather showed an inner strength and humility in their conversions of heart. It is those with weaker characters who lack grace and mercy, people who are too sensitive to the perceptions of others, and who fear being thought of as weak or compromising. This is the root of social justice. It has infected conservatism also—just look at the preening and squabbling between Republicans and "True Republicans" over Trump. The Kurt Schlichter–coined "TruCons" blast the right's bomb throwers and rightly point out that James and John didn't *stay* the sons of thunder. But guess what? Jesus didn't kick them out of his group of disciples, either. He didn't banish them. In fact, Jesus recruited them knowing full well their nature *and* their potential. He nurtured them, encouraged them, taught them, led them, *shepherded them* into the saints they ended their lives as. Again, "God doesn't call the equipped, he equips the called."

Let me be clear, and some out there need to hear this: We have enough bouncers within the Republican Party and the conservative movement. What we do not have enough of are *shepherds.* You don't like the inarticulate manner in which some other conservative stated an idea? Then offer constructive feedback born out of good faith. You think some young Republican group is too sassy and flashy and focuses more on stunts than substance? Then offer to mentor them. Encourage and shape their potential into something amazing. The Republican-conservative sphere isn't some exclusive club, it's a movement. If you treat it like an exclusive club it will die, and with it the advancement of freedom. Is massaging your ego worth that? Jesus didn't seem to think so.

The bit of good faith I have left would have run out by now were it not for the knowledge that bad people can turn good. Nothing feels quite so American as the great American comeback story. It's the point in the movie where the protagonist is at his lowest point, learns his true strength, and changes his fate. It's the moment during the boxing match when the judges have scored every round against him but he roars back for the knockout. We all root for him. We root for him because we've been there. We root for him because most of us know that low point of pain, of isolation. When he emerges victorious we feel proud. It's the type of story the country lives for: triumph after a fall.

It is not a story we often allow for anymore in our political culture because it requires the acknowledgement of redemption. Whether you're a Christian or not, on the right or the left, redemption is something you both need and deserve. I love what Nick Saban said about second chances when talking about former Michigan State and NFL wide receiver Muhsin Muhammad during a press conference in 2014:

There's always a lot of criticism out there when somebody does something wrong. Everybody wants to know, "How are you gonna punish the guy?" Alright, but there's not enough, for nineteen and twenty-year-old kids, people out there saying, "Why don't you give them another chance?"

Saban had given Muhammad such a second chance in 1993. While Muhammad was on probation for a marijuana arrest, campus police found a gun in the glove compartment of his car. Muhammad served time in jail. Many wanted him dropped from the Spartans. Saban, however, didn't join the accusers. He defended Muhammad:

Everybody in the school, every newspaper guy, everybody was killing the guy because he got in trouble and said there's no way he should be on our team. I didn't kick him off the team. I suspended him, I made him do stuff. He graduated from Michigan State. He played fifteen years in the league, he's the president of a company now, and he has seven children, and his oldest daughter goes to Princeton. So who was right? I feel strong about this now, really strong.[5]

If the purpose of a penalty is eventual redemption, a correction of action, is that purpose served by denying a second chance and the potential for redemption? Obviously, every situation is unique, but justice and grace *can* coexist.

There is certainly no room for both *schadenfreude* and grace. At the beginning of this book is a list of scripture and quotations that have influenced me the most in the past two years. One of those verses is Proverbs 24:17–18: "Do not gloat when your enemy falls; when they stumble, do not let your heart rejoice, or the Lord will see and disapprove and turn his wrath away from them."

I have a bit of experience with this. Back in 2010, CNN's Rick Sanchez was unhappy at being made fun of on *The Daily Show with Jon Stewart*. Sanchez unloaded while speaking on a satellite radio show hosted by Pete Dominick, former warm-up comedian for *The Daily Show*. Sanchez called Stewart a "bigot." Dominick asked him to elaborate:

Dominick: How is he a bigot?

Sanchez: I think he looks at the world through, his mom, who was a school teacher, and his dad, who was a physicist or something like that. Great, I'm so happy that he grew up in a suburban middle-class New Jersey home with everything you could ever imagine.

Dominick: What group is he bigoted towards?

Sanchez: Everybody else who's not like him. Look at his show, I mean, what does he surround himself with?[6]

Dominick pushed back by informing Sanchez that Stewart is Jewish and thus a minority himself, to which Sanchez responded:

I'm telling you that everybody who runs CNN is a lot like Stewart, and a lot of people who run all the other networks are a lot like Stewart, and to imply that somehow they, the people in this country who are Jewish, are an oppressed minority? *Yeah.*

Sanchez said the "yeah" was sarcastic, because "I can't see somebody not getting a job somewhere because they're Jewish." CNN promptly fired Sanchez. Noting the irony in Sanchez's suggesting that Jewish people control all the media and yet apparently not believing it enough himself to refrain from his slur of Stewart, I opined on Twitter: "I hope Rick Sanchez was fired by a Jew." Nearly ten years later, post-Parkland, and after I had appeared on a CNN town hall, "journalists" and leftist activists began scouring my timeline looking for dirt. Sadly for them, this tweet was the closest thing they could find. Everyone from *The Wrap* to Yahoo! reported the remark without context, claiming I was an anti-Semite and thus the organization with which I was associated at the time, the NRA, was anti-Semitic. Even Sarah Silverman got in on the act, pushing the narrative on social media. On the exact same day that I published my tweet, Conan O'Brien had tweeted: "CNN's Rick Sanchez said the Jews run CNN. Ah, so that's who we blame for Rick Sanchez."[7]

O'Brien wasn't in trouble with the rage mob because O'Brien wasn't challenging the rage mob's status quo. I was. They didn't come for him, but boy, did they come for me. Unfortunately truth wasn't on their side, and by the end of the day apologies and retractions piled up at my feet. Snopes fact-checked the story and was forced to correct the narrative. Many friends on the right and the left rallied to my defense. Were I obtuse, I might be silly enough to view this as a massive victory, a battle won. I didn't see it that way, however, because I saw it as something else: all of this happened because I was carried away by *schadenfreude*. To be clear, I still think Sanchez is a bigot, but did I have to be such a smart aleck? Perhaps noting the aforementioned unintended irony of his remark was enough.

When former Trump advisor Steve Bannon fell spectacularly from grace, I resisted the urge to crow about it on cable news, despite having known the man for years and having a very contentious history with him—one that caused me concern for his claimed influence on the president. I could have responded in many ways, but I chose restraint. I did so not out of any regard for Bannon, but out of consideration for Proverbs

24:17–18. Those who know me know it would take a direct edict from God to prevent me from celebrating such circumstances. But I'd be a hypocrite to celebrate. There is no justification for undermining one's own virtue by mirroring the malicious nature of the person whose downfall you felt was deserved.

I am no longer interested in investing in such resentments.

A writer on Second Amendment issues asked me how I deal with the daily trolls, insults, and threats. I replied that I ignore them and keep a laser focus. "I need to get better at that," my friend said.

"I've been doing this for over ten years and still haven't mastered it," I replied. "It takes a very long time. In developing thick skin, you also risk developing a hardened heart. Fight it all you can. There is power in vulnerability."

It's true. There is a brilliant line in the film *Mary Queen of Scots* uttered by Margot Robbie that showcases the struggle of leadership and responsibility—a struggle felt by anyone in such a position, but most acutely by women. Robbie, playing Queen Elizabeth I, stands on a parapet with a trusted advisor overlooking the English countryside. "I am more man than woman, now," she tells him. "The throne has made me so." It's a beautiful statement in both its brutal honesty and vulnerability. It's a remark that has less to do with stereotypical attributes of gender or sex and more to do with thickness of skin and detachment from emotionality. In the film, her service was a transformative sacrifice. You can lose heart even while fighting for good. You can so successfully inoculate yourself from the arrows that you no longer feel. It is monumentally difficult to find the balance between allowing yourself to feel the sting of blows but not allowing them to harden your heart. It's a daily struggle in certain positions. It's awful that it is part of politics and public discussion. Vulnerability is a universal struggle, neither male nor female. It's a doubled-edged sword, both a protection and a liability. Some misinterpret the acts of extending grace, finding common ground, or even showing that the insults sting as evidence of weakness. Nothing is further from the truth, and the only people selling you this line are those who stand to lose their grift to civility and reconciliation. It's good not to "go for the throat" in clashes of ideology; it's good to accept an apology, to give a second chance, to allow for the same redemption you've been given in more ways than one. Fight against every instinct you have to "harden up," so you don't lose your heart, your purpose, and your path forward. Fight smart: Vulnerability and grace are strengths of a different sort, harder won, harder to keep, harder to demonstrate. They violate our corrupt, barbaric human nature and make us feel exposed. The toughest warriors are the ones who know the time for a righteous fury and know the time for grace, for mercy over judgment. Grace is just as powerful a weapon as any. If you want to win, get used to fighting with it.

Notes

Chapter 1: American Tribalism

1. Veronica Stracqualursi, "Former Republican Congressman Warns Trump a 'Storm' Is Coming," CNN, August 14, 2019, https://www.cnn.com/2019/08/14/politics/mark-sanford-trump-2020-campaign/index.html.

2. Maggie Haberman, "Hillary Clinton, Just an Unrecognized Burrito Bowl Fan at Chipotle," *New York Times,* April 14, 2015, https://www.nytimes.com/2015/04/14/us/politics/on-the-road-hillary-clinton-stops-for-lunch-at-chipotle-and-goes-unrecognized.html.

3. D. L. Davis, "Clinton on the Hot Sear with Claim That Thousands Were Turned Away from the Polls in Wisconsin," Politifact, March 6, 2019, https://www.politifact.com/wisconsin/statements/2019/mar/06/hillary-clinton/clinton-hot-seat-claim-thousands-were-turned-away-/.

4. Brad Wilmouth, "CNN's Lockhart: Anyone Voting for Trump Is a 'Racist,'" NewsBusters, July 29, 2019, https://www.newsbusters.org/blogs/nb/brad-wilmouth/2019/07/29/cnns-lockhart-anyone-voting-trump-racist.

5. Emma Fantuzzo, "MSNBC's Chris Hayes: Trump Supporters Must Be 'Confronted and Destroyed,'" NewsBusters, July 19, 2019, https://www.newsbusters.org/blogs/nb/emma-fantuzzo/2019/07/19/msnbcs-chris-hayes-trump-supporters-must-be-confronted-and.

6. NewsBusters, "Dem Reads Letter on House Floor, Calls Trump Supporters Racists and 'Steeped in...," Facebook video, June 12, 2019, https://www.facebook.com/newsbusters/videos/dem-reads-letter-on-house-floor-calls-trump-supporters-racists-and-steeped-in-re/2231782133749627/.

7. Timothy Meads, "CNN Panel: White Women Trump Voters Are Racist and Heavily Invested in White Supremacy," Townhall, November 18, 2018 https://townhall.com/tipsheet/timothymeads/2018/11/18/cnn-panel-white-women-trump-voters-are-racist-and-heavily-invested-in-white-supr-n2536141.

8.   Tim Hains, "CNN's Tapper to Beto O'Rourke: Is It Racist To Vote for Donald Trump in 2020?" RealClear Politics, August 11, 2019, https://www.realclearpolitics.com/video/2019/08/11/cnns_tapper_to_beto_orourke_is_it_racist_to_vote_for_donald_trump.html.

9. Eugene Scott, "Anger at Being Labeled Racist Is the New 'Cultural Anxiety' for Trump Supporters," *Washington Post*, August 12, 2019, https://www.washingtonpost.com/politics/2019/08/12/anger-being-labeled-racist-is-new-cultural-anxiety-trump-supporters/.

10. Lisa DePaulo, "Thank You for Not Screaming," *GQ*, August 19, 2010, https://www.gq.com/story/joe-scarborough-msnbc-republican-morning-joe.

11.   "Trump a Racist? 32% of Democrats Say Any White Criticism of Politicians of Color Is Racist," Rasmussen Reports, July 17, 2019, http://www.rasmussenreports.com/public_content/politics/general_politics/july_2019/trump_a_racist_32_of_democrats_say_any_white_criticism_of_politicians_of_color_is_racist.

12. William J. Barber II, "The Racist History of Tipping," *Politico*, July 17, 2019, politi.co/2XTbzLi.

13. Will Carr (@WillCarr), ".@KNX1070 Reporting a Neighbor Did Not
    Call Authorities about Suspicious Activity Bc She Did Not Want To
    Racially Profile," Twitter, December 2, 2015, https://twitter.com/
    WillCarr/status/672265937194639362.

14. Jana Winter, "Army Ignored Warning Signs from Fort Hood Shooter,
    Former Classmate Says," Fox News, November 9, 2009, https://
    www.foxnews.com/story/
    army-ignored-warning-signs-from-fort-hood-shooter-former-
    classmate-says.

15. Alex Parker, "They're Great at Eating Their Own: 'Queer Eye' Star
    Cancels His Twitter Account Due to Hate over Calling Spicer 'a Good
    Guy,'" RedState, August 23, 2019, https://www.redstate.com/
    alexparker/2019/08/23/
    theyre-great-eating-queer-eye-star-cancels-twitter-account-due-hate-
    calling-spicer-good-guy/?utm_source=Twitter&utm_
    medium=social&utm_term=theyre-great-eating-queer-eye-star-
    cancels-twitter-account-due-hate-calling-spicer-good-guy&utm_
    content=0&utm_campaign=PostPromoterPro.

16. Nicole Weaver, "Sean Spicer Said 'Dancing with the Stars' Backlash
    for Karamo Brown Was 'So Nasty,'" Showbiz CheatSheet, September
    7, 2019, https://www.cheatsheet.com/entertainment/sean-spicer-said-
    dancing-with-the-stars-backlash-for-karamo-brown-was-so-nasty.
    html/.

17. David Marcus, "Announcement of a Mamet Revival on Broadway
    Gives Wokesters the Sads," The Federalist, September 18, 2019,
    https://thefederalist.com/2019/09/18/
    announcement-of-a-mamet-revival-on-broadway-gives-wokesters-the-
    sads/.

18. "Dem 2020 Diversity Not a Priority," Monmouth University Polling
    Institution, April 23, 2019, https://www.monmouth.edu/polling-
    institute/reports/MonmouthPoll_US_042319/.

19. William Jacobson, "The Purpose of Elizabeth Warren's Native
    American Plan Is To Help Warren's Presidential Campaign," Legal
    Insurrection, August 18, 2019, https://legalinsurrection.com/2019/08/
    the-purpose-of-elizabeth-warrens-native-american-plan-is-to-help-
    warrens-presidential-campaign/.

20. Valerie Richardson, "Elizabeth Warren's Story of Racist Grandparents Disputed by Cherokee Genealogist," *Washington Times,* March 11, 2018, https://www.washingtontimes.com/news/2018/mar/11/ elizabeth-warren-punts-dna-test-native-american-an/.

21. Jeffery Jones, "Trump Job Approval 43%; Ties Party Polarization Record," Gallup News, September 19, 2019, https://news.gallup.com/ poll/266906/trump-job-approval-ties-party-polarization-record.aspx.

22. Josh Feldman, "Mattis: Divisiveness a Threat to Democracy, We're in 'Constant Election Mode' Cheering against Each Other," MediaIte, September 2, 2019, https://www.mediaite.com/tv/ mattis-divisiveness-a-threat-to-democracy-were-in-constant-election- mode-cheering-against-each-other/.

Chapter 2: Socialist Wave

1. Diamond Siu, "Democratic Socialist of America Scored Wins in the Midterms. What's on Their Agenda?" NBC, December 8, 2018, https://www.nbcnews.com/politics/politics-news/ democratic-socialists-america-scored-wins-midterms-what-s-their- agenda-n941911.

2. Jerry Dunleavy, "AOC Blames Aide for 'Farting Cows' Green New Deal Document," *Washington Examiner,* March 30, 2019, https:// www.washingtonexaminer.com/news/ aoc-blames-staffer-for-controversial-green-new-deal-farting-cows- document.

3. Christina Tkacik, "Baltimore Mayor Catherine Pugh: 'You Can Smell the Rats,'" *Baltimore Sun,* September 12, 2018, https://www. baltimoresun.com/maryland/baltimore-city/bs-md-ci-pugh-smell-rats- 20180912-story.html.

4. Luke Broadwater and Ian Duncan, "'Neighborhoods Are Crying Out': Baltimore Has Highest Homicide Rate of U.S. Big Cities," *Baltimore Sun,* September 25, 2018, https://www.baltimoresun.com/ news/crime/bs-md-ci-fbi-data-20180924-story.html.

5. "Maryland Voter Registration: By the Numbers," *Baltimore Sun,* October 15, 2018, https://www.baltimoresun.com/politics/bs-md- voter-registration-by-the-numbers-20181015-story.html.

6. Emily Larsen, "Trump Attacks on Baltimore Could Help His Pennsylvania 2020 Strategy," *Washington Examiner,* July 30, 2019, https://www.washingtonexaminer.com/news/ trump-attacks-on-baltimore-could-help-his-pennsylvania-2020-strategy.

7. Milton Friedman, "Why Government Is the Problem," Hoover Institution, 1993, https://www.hoover.org/sites/default/files/uploads/ documents/friedman-government-problem-1993.pdf.

8. Leah Barkoukis, "Scott Presler and His Volunteer Team Took on LA This Weekend. The Results Are Incredible," Townhall, September 23, 2019, https://townhall.com/tipsheet/leahbarkoukis/2019/09/23/ scott-presler-la-n2553482.

9. 2 Thessalonians 3:10.

10. Michael Novak, "Social Justice: Not What You Think It Is," (Washington: The Heritage Foundation, December 29, 2009), https:// www.heritage.org/poverty-and-inequality/report/ social-justice-not-what-you-think-it.

11. Albin Krebs and Robert Thomas, "Notes on People; Some Disunity along the United Way," *New York Times,* September 19, 1981, https://www.nytimes.com/1981/09/19/nyregion/notes-on-people-some-disunity-along-the-united-way.html#pq=GTBW90.

12. "Socialism, Like Bernie Sanders, Is Anti-Charity," *Washington Examiner,* April 17, 2019, https://www.washingtonexaminer.com/ opinion/editorials/socialism-like-bernie-sanders-is-anti-charity.

13. Michael Tanner, "Less Welfare, More Charity," Cato Institute, August 20, 2014, https://www.cato.org/publications/commentary/ less-welfare-more-charity.

14. "Socialism, Like Bernie Sanders, Is Anti-Charity," *Washington Examiner,* April 17, 2019, https://www.washingtonexaminer.com/ opinion/editorials/socialism-like-bernie-sanders-is-anti-charity.

15. Curt Devine, "307,000 Veterans May Have Died Awaiting Veterans Affairs Health Care, Report Says," CNN, September 3, 2015, https:// www.cnn.com/2015/09/02/politics/va-inspector-general-report/index. html.

16. Alex Wayne, "Obamacare Website Costs Exceed $2 Billion, Study Finds," Bloomberg, September 24, 2014, https://www.bloomberg.com/news/articles/2014-09-24/obamacare-website-costs-exceed-2-billion-study-finds.

17. Eric Boehm, "Social Security Will Be Insolvent in 16 Years," Reason.com, April 22, 2019, https://reason.com/2019/04/22/social-security-will-be-insolvent-in-16-years/.

18. Jovan Williams, "ObamaCare Turns 6–$55 Billion in Waste, So Far," Investor's Business Daily, March 21, 2016, https://www.investors.com/politics/editorials/obamacare-turns-6-55-billion-in-waste-so-far/.

19. Kate Bernot, "Chick-fil-A Is Growing So Fast It Could Surpass Starbucks," The Takeout, June 18, 2019, https://thetakeout.com/chickfila-sales-growth-2018-restaurant-chains-starbucks-1835613469.

20. Kate Taylor, "Chick-fil-A Is Now the 3rd-Largest Restaurant Chain in America, and McDonald's and Starbucks Should Be Terrified," Business Insider, June 18, 2019, https://www.businessinsider.com/chick-fil-a-third-largest-restaurant-chain-in-america-2019-6.

21. Joshua Fruhlinger, "Chick-fil-A Isn't Just the Fastest Growing Chain, It's Poised for Acceleration," Thinknum.com, June 2019, https://media.thinknum.com/articles/chick-fil-a-growth-is-bucking-all-retail-and-fast-food-trends/.

22. Matthew McCreary, "Chick-fil-A Makes More Per Restaurant Than McDonald's Starbucks, and Subway Combined … and It's Closed on Sundays," Entrepreneur, June 2019, https://www.entrepreneur.com/article/320615.

23. "ACSI Restaurant Report 2018," American Customer Satisfaction Index, June 26, 2019, https://www.theacsi.org/news-and-resources/customer-satisfaction-reports/reports-2018/acsi-restaurant-report-2018.

24. "A Lesson in Customer Service from Chick-fil-A President Dan Cathy," SAS, https://www.sas.com/en_us/insights/articles/marketing/a-lesson-in-customer-service-from-chick-fil-a.html.

25. "About Remarkable Futures," Chicken Wire, Chick-fil-A, September 19, 2016, https://thechickenwire.chick-fil-a.com/News/About-Remarkable-Futures.

26. Barry Segal, "Chick-fil-A and 23 More Companies with Surprisingly Great 401(k) Plans," Yahoo Finance, August 19, 2019, https://finance.yahoo.com/news/chick-fil-23-more-companies-165854245.html.

27. Thomas Frohlich, *et al.*, "America's Best Companies To Work For," 24/7 Wall Street, August 10, 2015, https://247wallst.com/special-report/2015/08/10/the-best-companies-to-work-for/3/.

Chapter 3: Death of Nuance

1. "Fremont Police Tesla Near-Dead Battery Forces Officer Off Pursuit," CBS San Francisco, September 25, 2019, https://sanfrancisco.cbslocal.com/2019/09/25/fremont-police-tesla-out-of-electricity-pursuit/.

2. Elon Musk (@elonmusk), "Media Report Was False," Twitter, September 27, 2019, https://twitter.com/elonmusk/status/1177618032719319040.

3. Jeremy Owens (@jowens510), "Which Media Report, @elonmusk? The Original Report from @josephgeha16 Is Unassailable, and Fremont PD Statement Does Not Contradict Any Fact Included in That Story," Twitter, September 27, 2019, https://twitter.com/jowens510/status/1177649579770011648.

4. Serious Callers Only (@EthicsGradient), "Yep," Twitter, September 27, 2019, https://twitter.com/EthicsGradient/status/1177618937669832711.

5. TR (@nyctoph0bia17), "Same People Quick To Yell Fake News Cling To It When It Fits Their Narrative. Dana Loesch Is a Partisan Shill. What's New," Twitter, September 27, 2019, https://twitter.com/ZG1788/status/1177619292952678401.

6. Kieran (@Novaa_Bro), "So What Was the Purpose of Your Retweet? You Read the Title and Decided It's True Enough for You To Show Your Followers? This Is Why Cake News Is a Thing," Twitter, September 27, 2019, https://twitter.com/Novaa_Bro/status/1177650029508476928.

7. Amado Cruz (@AmadoCruz), "So You Just Deliberately Spread Falsehoods and When Found To Be False You Double Up?!" Twitter, September 27, 2019, https://twitter.com/AmadoCruz/status/1177664437035163648.

8. Tim Griepentrog (@Lego_naut), "So, Why Retweet Something That Was Wrong and Not Correct It?" Twitter, September 27, 2019, https://twitter.com/Lego_naut/status/1177665281726058497.

9. Omar Sanchez, "'Joker' Director Todd Phillips Rebuffs Criticism of Dark Tone: 'We Didn't Make the Movie To Push Buttons,'" The Wrap, September 25, 2019, https://www.thewrap.com/joker-director-todd-phillips-rebuffs-criticism-of-dark-tone-we-didnt-make-the-movie-to-push-buttons-exclusive/.

10. Heather Antos (@HeatherAntos), "Why the Joker Movie Is Problematic. Rachel Miller Nails It," Twitter, September 5, 2019, https://twitter.com/HeatherAntos/status/1169734410834448384.

11. Anthony Gramuglia, "Why Joker Is Sparking a Backlash over Its Portrayal of Incel Violence," CBR.com, September 5, 2019, https://www.cbr.com/joker-movie-backlash-explained/.

12. Richard Lawson, "*Joker* Review: Joaquin Phoenix Towers in a Deeply Troubling Origin Story," *Vanity Fair,* August 31, 2019, https://www.vanityfair.com/hollywood/2019/08/joker-review-joaquin-phoenix.

13. Owen Gleiberman, "Film Review: 'Joker,'" *Variety,* August 31, 2019, https://variety.com/2019/film/reviews/joker-review-joaquin-phoenix-todd-phillips-1203317033/.

14. David Rutz, "Dana Loesch Is Right: CNN Host Stood By as NRA Called 'Child Murderers,'" Free Beacon, February 23, 2018, https://freebeacon.com/issues/dana-loesch-is-right-cnn-host-stood-by-as-nra-called-child-murderers/.

15. Valerie Volcovici, " Greta Thunberg to U.S. Congress on Climate Change: 'Wake Up,'" Reuters, September 18, 2019, https://www.reuters.com/article/us-climate-change-thunberg-congress/greta-thunberg-to-congress-dont-listen-to-me-listen-to-the-scientists-idUSKBN1W31CM.

16. Robert Rapier, "Yes, the U.S. Leads All Countries in Reducing Carbon Emissions," *Forbes,* October 24, 2017, https://www.forbes.com/sites/rrapier/2017/10/24/yes-the-u-s-leads-all-countries-in-reducing-carbon-emissions/#289a51463535.

17. Robert Rapier, "China Emits More Carbon Dioxide Than the U.S. and EU Combined," *Forbes*, July 1, 2018, https://www.forbes.com/sites/rrapier/2018/07/01/china-emits-more-carbon-dioxide-than-the-u-s-and-eu-combined/#413c5a05628c.

18. Amir Vera, "Starbucks Apologizes after 6 Officers Say They Were Asked To Leave a Store in Arizona," CNN, July 8, 2019, https://www.cnn.com/2019/07/06/us/starbucks-apology-arizona-police-trnd/index.html.

19. Jamie Ross, "Man Killed Black Teen because Rap Music Made Him Feel 'Unsafe,'"Daily Beast, July 9, 2019, https://www.thedailybeast.com/michael-paul-adams-man-killed-black-teen-elijah-al-amin-because-rap-music-made-him-feel-unsafe.

Chapter 4: The History of Leftist Violence

1. Sheryl Gay Stolberg, "Ocasio-Cortez Calls Migrant Detention Centers 'Concentration Camps,' Eliciting Backlash," *New York Times*, June 18, 2019, https://www.nytimes.com/2019/06/18/us/politics/ocasio-cortez-cheney-detention-centers.html.

2. Alexandria Ocasio-Cortez (@AOC), "This video was from 1 year ago this week–before my primary & the Fox News cycle. I flew to the concentration camp where the Trump admin was keeping children they stole from their parents. Back then, I was voicing my conscience. I still am. #AbolishICE," June 18, 2019, 3:24 PM, https://twitter.com/AOC/status/1141109343171076109?ref_src=twsrc%5Etfw%7Ctwcamp%5Etweetembed%7Ctwterm%5E1141111031294570498&ref_url=https%3A%2F%2Ftwitchy.com%2Fsarahd-313035%2F2019%2F06%2F18%2Fcant-stop-wont-stop-aoc-tripling-down-on-her-concentration-camps-bs-is-proof-that-we-live-in-post-truth-times-video%2F.

3. Nolan Rappaport, "Bill Clinton's Attempts to Secure the Border Caused a Humanitarian Crisis," *The Hill*, November 23, 2018, https://thehill.com/opinion/immigration/417994-bill-clintons-attempts-to-secure-the-border-caused-a-humanitarian-crisis.

4. Annalisa Merelli, "Those Photos of Immigrant Children 'Caged' by the US? They're from 2014," *Quartz*, May 29, 2018, https://qz.com/1291470/photos-immigrant-children-detained-at-the-placement-center-in-2014/

5. Shelby Talcott, "Journalist Andy Ngo Attacked at Portland Rally. He Reportedly Sustained Injuries," *Daily Caller,* June 30, 2019, https://dailycaller.com/2019/06/30/andy-ngo-journalist-rally-injured/.

6. Brett T., "CNN's Jake Tapper 'Corrected' by Fellow Journalists After Calling Out Antifa for Violence," Twitchy, June 29, 2019, https://twitchy.com/brettt-3136/2019/06/29/cnns-jake-tapper-corrected-by-fellow-journalists-after-calling-out-antifa-for-violence/.

7. Emilie Raguso, "Eric Clanton Takes 3-Year Probation Deal in Berkeley Rally Bike Lock Assault Case," *Berkeleyside*, August 8, 2018, https://www.berkeleyside.com/2018/08/08/eric-clanton-takes-3-year-probation-deal-in-berkeley-rally-bike-lock-assault-case.

8. Ian Schwartz, "CNN's Chris Cuomo Defends Antifa: Attacks on Police, Journalists 'Not Equal' to Fighting Bigots," Real Clear Politics, August 14, 2018, https://www.realclearpolitics.com/video/2018/08/14/cnn_chris_cuomo_defends_antifa_attacks_on_police_journalists_not_equal_to_fighting_bigots.html.

9. Paul Kengor, "Charles Manson and the Weather Underground," *The American Spectator,* November 21, 2017, https://spectator.org/charles-manson-and-the-weather-underground/.

10. Dohrn served seven months in prison for refusing to testify against one of her radical comrades.

11. "Trump Protesters Smash Windows of Cars, Businesses," ABC News, November 11, 2016, https://www.youtube.com/watch?v=nKMSWAGTU0E.

12. Joseph Weber, "Hundreds of Protesters Arrested in Inauguration Day Clashes," Fox News, January 20, 2017, https://www.foxnews.com/politics/hundreds-of-protesters-arrested-in-inauguration-day-clashes.

13. Justin Wm. Moyer, "'That's Not Somebody's Honda': Owner of Limo Torched on Inauguration Day Unsure if Insurance Will Cover

Damages," *Washington Post*, January 25, 2017, https://www.washingtonpost.com.

14. Chase Stephens, "Video Shows Trump Supporter Knocked Out and Taunted by Violent Portland Airport Protesters," Daily Wire, January 30, 2017, https://www.dailywire.com/news/video-shows-trump-supporter-knocked-out-and-chase-stephens.

15. Kevin Daley, "Madonna Said She Thought of Blowing up the White House. Is That Illegal?" Daily Caller, January 23, 2017, https://dailycaller.com/2017/01/23/madonna-said-she-thought-of-blowing-up-the-white-house-is-that-illegal/.

16. "More Than 12,000 Tweets Have Called for Trump's Assassination Since the Inauguration," *Daily Mail*, February 3, 2017, https://www.dailymail.co.uk/news/article-4189124/More-12-000-tweets-call-Trump-s-assassination.html#ixzz4k0h0zXDl.

17. Ian Schwartz, "Loretta Lynch on Trump Protests: People Have Marched, Bled and Died to Make a Difference," Real Clear Politics, March 7, 2017, https://www.realclearpolitics.com/video/2017/03/07/loretta_lynch_on_trump_protests_people_have_marched_bled_and_died_to_make_a_difference.html.

18. Allison Stanger, "Understanding the Angry Mob at Middlebury That Gave Me a Concussion," *New York Times*, March 13, 2017, https://www.nytimes.com/2017/03/13/opinion/understanding-the-angry-mob-that-gave-me-a-concussion.html.

19. Douglas Ernst, "Rob Reinter Proclaims 'All Out War' Ongoing To 'Save Democracy' from Fox News, Trump," *Washington Times,* June 26, 2017, https://www.washingtontimes.com/news/2017/jun/26/rob-reiner-proclaims-all-out-war-ongoing-to-save-d/.

20. Jake Gibson, "Scalise Shooter James Hodgkinson Had Lost of Republican Lawmakers' Names," Fox News, June 16, 2017, https://www.foxnews.com/us/scalise-shooter-james-hodgkinson-had-list-of-republican-lawmakers-names.

21. Douglas Ernst, "HuffPo Scrubs 'Ultimate Punishment' Trump Piece After Scalise, GOP Shooting," *Washington Times*, June 15, 2017,

https://www.washingtontimes.com/news/2017/jun/15/
huffpo-scrubs-jason-fullers-ultimate-punishment-tr/.

22. Hank Berrien, "Moms Demand Action Leader Charged After
    Screaming Obscenities at Teenage Girl Wearing Trump T-Shirt,"
    Daily Wire, https://www.dailywire.com/news/
    moms-demand-action-leader-charged-after-screaming-hank-berrien.

23. "Several Shots Fired at Truck Flying 'Make America Great Again'
    Flag on I-465," Fox59, June 15, 2017, https://fox59.com/2017/06/15/
    several-shots-fired-at-truck-carrying-make-america-great-again-flag-
    on-i-465/.

24. Melissa Quinn, "HUD Secretary Ben Carson's Home Vandalized
    with Anti-Trump Rhetoric," *Washington Examiner*, August 16, 2017,
    https://www.washingtonexaminer.com/hud-secretary-ben-carsons-
    home-vandalized-with-anti-trump-rhetoric/article/2631755.

25. David Harsanyi, "There Is No 'Surge' in Right-Wing Violence,"
    Creators, November 30, 2018, https://www.creators.com/read/david-
    harsanyi/11/18/there-is-no-surge-in-right-wing-violence.

26. Fred Barbash, "Federal Appeals Court Orders Resentencing of Man
    Who Assaulted Sen. Rand Paul," *Washington Post*, September 9,
    2019, https://www.washingtonpost.com/national-security/federal-
    appeals-court-orders-resentencing-of-man-who-assaulted-sen-rand-
    paul/2019/09/09/9c9163e2-d331-11e9-86ac-0f250cc91758_story.
    html.

27. Kevin McCarthy (@kevinomccarthy), "Targeting and Harassing
    Americans Because of Their Political Beliefs Is Shameful and
    Dangerous," Twitter, August 6, 2019, 3:42 p.m., https://twitter.com/
    kevinomccarthy/status/1158840773435154433?lang=en.

28. Sam J., "And So It Begins: Woman Outed by Joaquin Castro as a
    Trump Donor Already Receiving Threatening Voicemails," Twitchy,
    August 9, 2019, https://twitchy.com/samj-3930/2019/08/09/
    and-so-it-begins-woman-outed-by-joaquin-castro-as-a-trump-donor-
    already-receiving-threatening-voicemails/.

29. Ronn Blitzer, "Joaquin Castro Facing Backlash from All Sides for
    Posting Trump Donor Information," Fox News, August 7, 2019,
    https://www.foxnews.com/politics/
    castro-getting-called-out-from-both-sides-after-outing-trump-donors.

30. Michael Del Moro, "Stephen Ross—chair of the company that owns SoulCycle and Equinox—"freaked out" at the backlash to his upcoming Trump fundraiser and privately expressed concerns, but ultimately decided to move forward anyway, @jonathanvswan reported on @Morning_Joe," August 9, 2019, 4:06 AM, https://twitter.com/MikeDelMoro/status/1159783061229379584.

31. Kevin Lewis, "'I'll Wear It Again': Duo Allegedly Attacks, Robs Immigrant for Wearing MAGA Baseball Cap," ABC7, April 15, 2019, https://wjla.com/news/local/two-charged-in-assault-of-man-who-says-he-was-attacked-for-wearing-maga-hat.

32. Maria Perez, "Donald Trump MAGA Hat Attacks, Intolerance: List of Reported Incidents Against People Wearing President's Caps," *Newsweek*, March 11, 2019, https://www.newsweek.com/criminal-acts-trump-maga-hats-1357179.

33. Perez, "Donald Trump MAGA Hat Attacks."

34. Joe Tacopino, "New Jersey Teen Arrested for Beating Elderly Man Over MAGA Hat," *New York Post*, February 27, 2019, https://nypost.com/2019/02/27/new-jersey-teen-arrested-for-beating-elderly-man-over-maga-hat/.

35. "Woman Charged With Attacking Falmouth Man Wearing MAGA Hat Taken Into ICE Custody," CBS Boston, February 26, 2019, https://boston.cbslocal.com/2019/02/26/president-trump-make-america-great-again-hat-confrontation-rosiane-santos-ice/.

36. "Former Grijalva Staffer Misses Court Hearing, Launched Unprovoked Attack on Trump Supporter," Arizona Independent Daily News Network, March 4, 2019, https://arizonadailyindependent.com/2019/03/04/grijalva-staffer-misses-court-hearing-for-maga-hat-assault-charges/.

37. Jason Murdock, "Kansas Vans Employee Fired After Allegedly Swearing at Teen Wearing MAGA Hat: 'Sure He's Heard It Before,'" *Newsweek*, February 2, 2019, https://www.newsweek.com/vans-kansas-make-america-great-again-maga-hat-teenager-overland-park-oak-park-1335143.

38. "Texas Man Arrested for Attack on Boy Wearing Trump Hat," BBC News, July 6, 2018, https://www.bbc.com/news/world-us-canada-44745676.

39. Ryan Saavedra, "EXCLUSIVE: Cheesecake Factory Employees Attack Black Man for Wearing MAGA Hat, Witnesses Say," Daily Wire, May 14, 2018, https://www.dailywire.com/news/30628/exclusive-cheesecake-factory-employees-attack-ryan-saavedra.

40. Allyssa Milano (@Alyssa_Milano), "The red MAGA hat is the new white hood. Without white boys being able to empathize with other people, humanity will continue to destroy itself. #FirstThoughtsWhenIWakeUp," January 20, 2019, 8:19 AM, https://twitter.com/Alyssa_Milano/status/1087021713651421184.

41. Tyler McCarthy, "Alyssa Milano Doubles Down on Calling Trump MAGA Hats 'The New White Hood,'" Fox News, January 24, 2019, https://www.foxnews.com/entertainment/alyssa-milano-doubles-down-on-calling-trump-maga-hats-the-new-white-hood.

42. Zack Beauchamp, "The Real Politics Behind the Covington Catholic Controversy, Explained," Vox, January 23, 2019, https://www.vox.com/policy-and-politics/2019/1/23/18192831/covington-catholic-maga-hat-native-american-nathan-phillips.

43. Isaac Bailey, "Why Trump's MAGA Hats Have Become a Potent Symbol of Racism," CNN, March 12, 2019, https://www.cnn.com/2019/01/21/opinions/maga-hat-has-become-a-potent-racist-symbol-bailey/index.html.

44. Zack Ford, "On MAGA Hats … Would You Choose a Hat Over a Friend?" July 5, 2019, https://zackford.substack.com/p/on-maga-hats.

45. Kyle Smith, "Dave Chappelle Goes After Jussie Smollett," National Review, August 29, 2019, https://www.nationalreview.com/corner/dave-chappelle-goes-after-jussie-smollett/.

46. Greg P., "'LOL, Get Rekt A**hole': A Former Associate DNC Comms Director Got Kicked Out of a D.C. Restaurant After Harassing a MAGA-hat 'Nazi'," Twitchy, July 5, 2019, https://twitchy.com/gregp-3534/2019/07/05/lol-get-rekt-ahole-a-former-associate-dnc-comms-director-got-kicked-out-of-a-d-c-restaurant-after-harassing-a-maga-hat-nazi/.

47. Ben Smith (@BenSmithDC), "Every day I see hundreds of tourists walking through my area…. A few days ago, I sat down to grab a quick bite before heading to a housewarming party … ," Twitter, https://twitter.com/BenSmithDC/status/1147174081042833408.

48. ABC News (@ABC), "'Mean pettiness has overtaken our politics,' Joe Biden says. 'If you notice, I get criticized for saying anything nice about a Republican. Folks, that's not who we are.'" March 12, 2019, 7:08 AM, https://twitter.com/ABC/status/1105470709935988737?ref_src= twsrc%5Etfw%7Ctwcamp%5Etweetembed%7Ctwterm%5E110547 0709935988737&ref_url=https%3A%2F%2Fdailycaller. com%2F2019%2F03%2F12%2Fbiden-nice-things-republicans-pence%2F.

49. Chris Mills Rodrigo, "Trump Accuses Pelosi of 'Racist Statement' for Saying MAGA Means 'Make America White Again,'" *The Hill*, July 15, 2019, https://thehill.com/homenews/ administration/453108-trump-hits-pelosi-for-racist-statement-saying-maga-means-make-america.

50. Peggy Noonan, "Mind Your Manners, Says Edith Wharton," *Wall Street Journal,* August 22, 2019, https://www.wsj.com/articles/ mind-your-manners-says-edith-wharton-11566510905.

Chapter 5: Milkshake Ducks and Rage Mobs

1. Aaron Calvin, "Meet Carson King, the 'Iowa Legend' Who's Raised More Than $1 Million for Charity Off of a Sign Asking for Beer Money," *Des Moines Register,* September 24, 2019, https://www. desmoinesregister.com/story/sports/college/iowa-state/ football/2019/09/24/ meet-carson-king-whos-raised-over-1-million-charity-asking-beer-money-childrens-hospital-tweet/2427538001/.

2. Des Moines Register (@DMRegister), "A statement from our editor:," Twitter, 11:48 p.m., September 24, 2019, https://twitter.com/DMRegister/ status/1176705031468457985.

3. Staff Writer, "Carson King Apologizes After 'Hurtful and Embarrassing' Tweet Surfaces," WHO TV, September 24, 2019, https://whotv. com/2019/09/24/ carson-king-apologizes-after-hurtful-and-embarrassing-tweet-surfaces/.

4. Gillian Branstetter, "What Chewbacca Mom's Rise to Fame Tells Us About Race in This Country," Daily Dot, June 3, 2016, https://www.dailydot.com/via/what-chewbacca-mom-tells-us-about-race/.

5. Sean O'Neal, "And Lo, the World Began to Turn Against Chewbacca Mom," AV Club, July 12, 2016, https://news.avclub.com/and-lo-the-world-began-to-turn-against-chewbacca-mom-1798249350.

6. "'Chewbacca Mom' Sings Michael Jackson's 'Heal the World' After Dallas Shooting," WUSA9, July 10, 2016, https://www.wusa9.com/article/news/local/
chewbacca-mom-sings-michael-jacksons-heal-the-world-after-dallas-shooting/65-268861170.

7. Ashley Weatherford, "Kayla Newman, the Woman Who Invented 'On Fleek', On Building a Beauty Empire," The Cut, October 25, 2017, https://www.thecut.com/2017/10/kayla-newman-peaches-monroee-on-fleek-extensions-interview.html.

8. Erin McLaughlin, "'On Fleek'" Inventor Kayla Newman AKA Peaches Monroe On Her Beauty Line," *Teen Vogue*, March 9, 2017, https://www.teenvogue.com/story/
on-fleek-inventor-kayla-newman-aka-peaches-monroe-on-her-beauty-line.

9. CNN (@CNN), "Ken Bone says he wore the red sweater as a plan B to the debate because he 'split the seat of my pants wide open,'" Twitter, 7:38 a.m., October 10, 2016, https://twitter.com/CNN/status/785489769929273344.

10. Kaleb Roedel, "Nuggets Watch: NASCAR Driver to Feature #NuggsForCarter Decal in Sunday's Race," KRNV News 4, April 20, 2017, https://mynews4.com/news/local/
nuggets-watch-nascar-driver-to-feature-nuggsforcarter-decal-in-sundays-race.

11. Lizzy Acker, "#MeNeither YouTube Videos Create Backlash for Portland Coffee Company," *The Oregonian*, January 10, 2019, https://www.oregonlive.com/news/2019/01/part-owner-of-portland-coffee-company-questions-accounts-of-sexual-assault-survivors-on-youtube.html.

12. NewsOne Staff, "Twitter Slams Kevin Hart Over His Reaction to Lil Nas X Saying He Was Taught to Hate Being Gay," News One, September 4, 2019, https://newsone.com/playlist/twitter-kevin-hart-lil-nas-x/.

13. Stephen Daw, "A Complete Time of Kevin Hart's Oscar-Hosting Controversy, from Tweets to Apologies," Billboard, January 10, 2019, https://www.billboard.com/articles/events/oscars/8492982/kevin-hart-oscar-hosting-controversy-timeline.

14. Kevin Hart (@KevinHart4real), "I have made the choice to step down from hosting this year's Oscar's.... this is because I do not want to be a distraction on a night that should be celebrated by so many amazing talented artists. I sincerely apologize to the LGBTQ community for my insensitive words from my past." Twitter, 9:01 p.m., December 6, 2018, https://twitter.com/KevinHart4real/status/1070906075812118529.

15. TheEllenShow, "Kevin Hart Opens Up About Oscars Controversy," YouTube video, 6:37, January 4, 2019, https://www.youtube.com/watch?v=uXtlGdPenbc&feature=youtu.be.

16. TheEllenShow, "Ellen Reveals She Called the Academy to Help Re-Hire Kevin Hart as Oscars Host," YouTube video, 6:59, January 4, 2019, https://www.youtube.com/watch?v=VWlAIbxoLmc.

17. Jon Ronson, "How One Stupid Tweet Ruined Justine Sacco's Life," New York Times, February 12, 2015, https://www.nytimes.com/2015/02/15/magazine/how-one-stupid-tweet-ruined-justine-saccos-life.html.

18. Sam Biddle, "Justine Sacco Is Good at Her Job, and How I Came to Peace With Her," Gawker, December 20, 2014, https://gawker.com/justine-sacco-is-good-at-her-job-and-how-i-came-to-pea-1653022326.

19. Zack Sharf, "'Green Book' Writer Nick Vallelonga Supported Trump's Claim That New Jersey Muslims Cheered 9/11," Indie Wire, January 9, 2019, https://www.indiewire.com/2019/01/green-book-nick-vallelonga-tweet-support-donald-trump-new-jersey-muslims-cheered-9-11-1202034085/.

20. Trilby Beresford, "'Green Book' Writer Nick Vallelonga Apologizes for Resurfaced Anti-Muslim Tweet," Hollywood Reporter, January 10, 2019, https://www.hollywoodreporter.com/news/green-book-writer-nick-vallelonga-apologizes-anti-muslim-tweet-1175361.

21. Ben Shapiro, "Yes, Some American Muslims Did Celebrate 9/11. The Media Stepped on Another Trump-Brand Rake," Daily Wire, November 24, 2019, https://www.dailywire.com/news/1338/yes-some-american-muslims-did-celebrate-911-media-ben-shapiro.

22. Karen Templer, "2019: My Year of Color," Fringe Association, January 7, 2019, https://fringeassociation.com/2019/01/07/2019-my-year-of-color/.

23. Katherine Jebsen Moore, "A Witch-Hunt on Instagram," Quillette, February 17, 2019, https://quillette.com/2019/02/17/a-witch-hunt-on-instagram/.

24. Jaya Saxena, "The Knitting Community is Reckoning with Racism," Vox, February 25, 2019, https://www.vox.com/the-goods/2019/2/25/18234950/knitting-racism-instagram-stories.

25. Katherine Moore, "A Witch-Hunt on Instagram," Quillette, February 17, 2019, https://quillette.com/2019/02/17/a-witch-hunt-on-instagram/.

26. Kassy Cho, "This Teen Wore a Traditional Chinese Dress to Prom and Caused a Huge Controversy," BuzzFeed News, May 1, 2018, https://www.buzzfeednews.com/article/kassycho/keziah-daum-prom-qipao-cheongsam.

27. Tony Mauro, "Brett Kavanaugh's 'Friends': Inside Ex-Kirkland Partner's SCOTUS Briefs," *National Law Journal*, July 23, 2018, https://www.law.com/nationallawjournal/2018/07/23/brett-kavanaughs-friends-inside-ex-kirkland-partners-scotus-briefs.

28. Paul Bedard, "Kavanaugh's Daughters Rushed Out of Chaotic, 'Hot' Hearing," *Washington Examiner*, September 4, 2018, https://www.washingtonexaminer.com/washington-secrets/brett-kavanaughs-daughters-rushed-out-of-hearing.

29. Yaron Steinburch, "Friend of Ford Told FBI She Was Pressured into Altering Statement," *New York Post*, October 5, 2018, https://nypost.com/2018/10/05/friend-of-ford-told-fbi-she-was-pressured-into-altering-statement/.

30. Janet Hook, "Interest in Midterms Surges, Along With Trump Approval Rating," *Wall Street Journal*, October 21, 2018, https://www.wsj.com/articles/interest-in-midterms-surges-boosting-trump-approval-rating-1540126920.

31. Philip Wegmann, "Kavanaugh Vote Was Supremely Helpful to Joe Manchin," *Washington Examiner*, October 23, 2018, https://www.washingtonexaminer.com/opinion/kavanaugh-vote-was-supremely-helpful-to-joe-manchin.

32. Tiana Lowe, "Data: Of Course the Kavanaugh Hearings Hurt #MeToo," *Washington Examiner*, April 17, 2019, https://www.washingtonexaminer.com/opinion/data-of-course-the-brett-kavanaugh-hearings-hurt-metoo.

33. K. Allan Blume, "'Guilty as Charged,' Dan Cathy Says of Chick-fil-A's Stand on Faith," Biblical Recorder, July 2, 2012, https://brnow.org/News/July-2012/Guilty-as-charged-Dan-Cathy-says-of-Chick-fil-A.

34. Tim Fitzsimons, "U.K.'s First Chick-fil-A to Close Following LGBTQ Protests," NBC News, October 21, 2019, https://www.nbcnews.com/feature/nbc-out/u-k-s-first-chick-fil-close-following-lgbtq-protests-n1069621.

35. Jefferson Graham, "Chick-Fil-A Won't Be Landing at Buffalo Airport," USA Today, April 1, 2019, https://www.usatoday.com/story/money/2019/04/01/buffalo-airport-says-no-new-airport-location-Chick-fil-A/3336958002/.

36. Michelle Lou and Veronica Stracqualursi, "The Texas Attorney General Is Investigating San Antonio for Banning Chick-fil-A from Its Airport," CNN, March 29, 2019, https://www.cnn.com/2019/03/29/politics/texas-san-antonio-airport-chick-fil-a-investigation/index.html.

37. Dennis Foley, "Smoke Shack, Spurs and Others Coming to San Antonio International; Chick-Fil-A Blocked," KTSA, March 21, 2019, https://www.ktsa.com/smoke-shack-spurs-and-other-coming-to-san-antonio-international-Chick-fil-A-blocked/

38. Cameron Sperance, "EXCLUSIVE: Chick-fil-A to Stop Donations to Charities with Anti-LGBT Views," Bisnow Media, November 18, 2019, https://www.bisnow.com/national/news/retail/exclusive-amid-global-expansion-and-lgbt-pushback-Chick-fil-A-changes-charitable-giving-structure-101818.

Chapter 6: The Death of Redemption

1. Maggie Serota, "Norm Macdonald's Opinion on #MeToo Is Exactly What You'd Expect," Spin, September 11, 2018, https://www.spin.com/2018/09/norm-macdonald-me-too-interview-quotes/.

2. Krystie Lee Yandoli, "Norm Macdonald Was Dropped from 'The Tonight Show' after Defending Roseanne Barr and Louis C. K.," BuzzFeed, September 12, 2018, https://www.buzzfeednews.com/article/krystieyandoli/norm-macdonald-roseanne-barr-louis-ck.

3. Tom Gilson, "A Better Way Than Shaming: Why the Culture Wars Need the Gospel, Part 2," The Stream, September 12, 2019, https://stream.org/better-than-shame-why-the-culture-wars-need-the-gospel-part-2/.

4.   Tom Gilson, "Shame on Everyone! Or, Why the Culture Wars Need the Gospel (Part 1)," *The Stream*, September 7, 2019, https://stream.org/shame-culture-wars-need-gospel-1/.

5.   Michael W. Chapman, "Neo-Con Jennifer Rubin: 'We Have to Collectively, in Essence, Burn Down the Republican Party,'" CNS News, August 27, 2019, https://www.cnsnews.com/blog/michael-w-chapman/neo-con-jennifer-rubin-we-have-collectively-essence-burn-down-republican.

6.   CNN Wire Service, "Officials: 12-Year-Old Who Claimed White Classmates Cut Her Dreadlocks Admits She Made the Story Up," Fox 6 Now, September 30, 2019, https://fox6now.com/2019/09/30/officials-12-year-old-who-claimed-white-classmates-cut-her-dreadlocks-admits-she-made-the-story-up/.

7.   Ed Morrissey, "Mika: 'I Apologize to Everyone' for My 'Butt-Boy' Comment," *Hot Air* (blog), December 14, 2018, https://hotair.com/archives/ed-morrissey/2018/12/14/mika-apologize-everyone-butt-boy-comment/.

8.   Chris Cassidy and Matt Stout, "Activists Put Heat on GBH to Oust Donor, Board Giant," *Boston Herald*, October 4, 2013, https://web.archive.org/web/20141208052702/http://www.bostonherald.com/news_opinion/local_coverage/2013/10/activists_put_heat_on_gbh_to_oust_donor_board_giant.

9.   Robin Pogrebin, "David H. Koch to Give $100 Million to Theater," *New York Times*, July 10, 2018, https://www.nytimes.com/2008/07/10/arts/10linc.html; Miriam Kreinin Souccar, "It's a Philanthropy Thing," Crain's New York Business, June 27, 2010, https://www.crainsnewyork.com/article/20100627/ANNIVERSARY/100619869/it-s-a-philanthropy-thing.

10. "Celebrating David Koch's Life and Legacy," Koch Newsroom, August 23, 2019, https://news.kochind.com/news/2019/david-koch-koch-industries.

11. Bradley Evans, "Hollywood Star Ron Perlman Leads the Way as Leftists Celebrate David Koch's Death," The Western Journal, August 24, 2019, https://www.westernjournal.com/hollywood-star-ron-perlman-leads-way-leftists-celebrate-david-kochs-death/.

12. Jennifer Emily et al., "Amber Guyger Convicted of Murder for Killing Botham Jean; Sentencing Phase To Continue Wednesday," *Dallas Morning News,* October 1, 2019, https://www.dallasnews.com/news/courts/2019/10/01/jurors-begin-second-day-deliberations-amber-guygers-murder-trial/.

Chapter 7: The Media's Role

1. Joseph A. Wulfsohn, "After Smearing Dana Loesch, the Media Cannot Let These Parkland Students Go Unchallenged," Mediaite, February 27, 2018, https://www.mediaite.com/online/after-smearing-dana-loesch-the-media-cannot-let-these-parkland-students-go-unchallenged/.

2. Sarah D., "'Sit Down': Dana Loesch Is Not Buying Brian Stelter's Righteous Indignation Over Ex-WH Officials Landing Plum Gigs [Video]," Twitchy, August 22, 2019, https://twitchy.com/sarahd-313035/2019/08/22/sit-down-dana-loesch-is-not-buying-brian-stelters-righteous-indignation-over-ex-wh-officials-landing-plum-gigs/.

3. Thomas E. Patterson, "News Coverage of Donald Trump's First 100 Days," Shorenstein Center on Media, Politics and Public Policy, May 18, 2017, https://shorensteincenter.org/news-coverage-donald-trumps-first-100-days/?utm_source=POLITICO.EU&utm_campaign=ab6d830a9d-EMAIL_CAMPAIGN_2017_05_19&utm_medium=email&utm_term=0_10959edeb5-ab6d830a9d-189799085.

4. Paul Bedard, "Pew: Trump Media Three Times More Negative Than for Obama, Just 5 Percent Positive," *Washington Examiner,* December 27, 2017, https://www.washingtonexaminer.com/pew-trump-media-three-times-more-negative-than-for-obama-just-5-percent-positive.

5. Jane C. Timm, "There's No Evidence for Trump's Biden-Ukraine Accusations. What Really Happened?" NBC News, September 25, 2019, https://www.nbcnews.com/politics/2020-election/there-s-no-evidence-trump-s-biden-ukraine-accusations-what-n1057851.

6. Nic Rowan, "Flashback: Joe Biden Got Angry When Obama Campaign Vetted Hunter Biden," Washington Free Beacon, September 25, 2019, https://freebeacon.com/politics/flashback-joe-biden-got-angry-when-obama-campaign-vetted-hunter-biden/.

7. Rich Noyes and Mike Ciandella, "2017: The Year the News Media Went to War against a President," NewsBusters, January 16, 2018, https://www.newsbusters.org/blogs/nb/rich-noyes/2018/01/16/2017-year-news-media-went-war-against-president.

8. Rich Noyes, "Six Trump Accomplishments the Networks Ignored in 2017," NewsBusters, January 17, 2018, https://www.newsbusters.org/blogs/nb/rich-noyes/2018/01/17/six-trump-accomplishments-networks-ignored-2017.

9. Glenn Greenwald, "Beyond BuzzFeed: The 10 Worst, Most Embarrassing U.S. Media Failures on the Trump-Russia Story," The Intercept, January 20, 2019, https://theintercept.com/2019/01/20/beyond-buzzfeed-the-10-worst-most-embarrassing-u-s-media-failures-on-the-trumprussia-story/.

10. Editorials, "Washington Post Caught Red Handed Peddling Anti-Trump Fake News," *Investor's Business Daily*, September 18, 2018, https://www.investors.com/politics/editorials/washington-post-fake-news-passports-media-bias/.

11. Peter Hasson, "CNN Reporter Falsely Claims Republicans Funded Trump-Russia Dossier [VIDEO]," The Daily Caller, December 26, 2017, https://dailycaller.com/2017/12/26/cnn-reporter-falsely-claims-republicans-funded-trump-russia-dossier-video/?utm_source=site-share.

12. Manu Raju and Jeremy Herb, "Email Pointed Trump Campaign to WikiLeaks Documents," CNN, December 8, 2017, https://www.cnn.com/2017/12/08/politics/email-effort-give-trump-campaign-wikileaks-documents/index.html.

13. Jeff Pegues, "House Intel Investigates Trump Jr. Email Involving Documents Hacked during Campaign," CBS News, December 8, 2017, https://webcache.googleusercontent.com/search?q=cache:JQQiz AodBAMJ:https://www.cbsnews.com/news/house-intel-investigates-trump-jr-email-involving-documents-hacked-during-campaign/+&cd =1&hl=en&ct=clnk&gl=us.

14. Becket Adams, "The Detail You Might Have Missed about ABC News Disciplining the Reporter Who Bungled the Michael Flynn News," *Washington Examiner*, December 5, 2017, https://www. washingtonexaminer.com/ the-detail-you-might-have-missed-about-abc-news-disciplining-the-reporter-who-bungled-the-michael-flynn-news.

15. *Newsweek* (@Newsweek), "Fact check: No, the Clintons were not paid millions by Russia," Twitter, October 19, 2017, 9:50 p.m., https:// twitter.com/Newsweek/status/921191757022355456.

16. Jo Becker and Mike McIntire, "Cash Flowed to Clinton Foundation Amid Russian Uranium Deal," *New York Times*, April 23, 2015, https://www.nytimes.com/2015/04/24/us/cash-flowed-to-clinton-foundation-as-russians-pressed-for-control-of-uranium-company. html?_r=1; Louis Nelson, "What You Need to Know about Clinton and the Uranium One Deal," *Politico*, November 14, 2017, https:// www.politico.com/story/2017/11/14/ hillary-clinton-uranium-one-deal-russia-explainer-244895.

17. Megan Brenan, "Americans' Trust in Mass Media Edges Down to 41%," Gallup, September 26, 2019, https://news.gallup.com/ poll/267047/americans-trust-mass-media-edges-down.aspx.

18. Jonathan Strong, "Documents Show Media Plotting to Kill Stories about Rev. Jeremiah Wright," The Daily Caller, July 20, 2010, https:// dailycaller.com/2010/07/20/ documents-show-media-plotting-to-kill-stories-about-rev-jeremiah-wright/.

19. Jonathan Strong, "Liberal Journalists Suggest Government Censor Fox News," The Daily Caller, July 21, 2010, https://dailycaller. com/2010/07/21/ liberal-journalists-suggest-government-shut-down-fox-news/.

20. Ibid.
21. Chad Brady, "Raw Journalist Emails: Do Tea Party Members 'Parallel' Nazis?" July 29, 2010, The Daily Caller, https://dailycaller.com/2010/07/29/raw-journolist-emails-do-tea-party-members-parallel-nazis/.
22. Kenneth P. Vogel and Jeremy W. Peters, "Trump Allies Target Journalists over Coverage Deemed Hostile to White House," *New York Times*, August 26, 2019, https://www.nytimes.com/2019/08/25/us/politics/trump-allies-news-media.html
23. Paul Farhi, "Said Something You'd Like to Forget? CNN's Andrew Kaczynski Won't Let It Go," *Washington Post*, August 15, 2018, https://washingtonpost.com/lifestyle/style/said-something-youd-like-to-forget-cnns-andrew-kaczynski-wont-let-it-go/2018/08/15/4a863526-8f82-11e8-bcd5-9d911c784c38_story.html.
24. Andrew Kaczynski, "How CNN Found the Reddit User behind the Trump Wrestling GIF," CNN, July 5, 2017, https://www.cnn.com/2017/07/04/politics/kfile-reddit-user-trump-tweet/index.html.
25. CNN (@CNN), "A Florida Woman Who Ran a Trump Supporters Page That Unwittingly Promoted a Russian-Coordinated Event on Facebook Says She Doesn't Believe That She Was Influenced by Kremlin-Linked Trolls," Twitter, February 20, 2018, 9:14 p.m., https://twitter.com/cnn/status/966134015337140229?lang=en.
26. Kevin Poulsen, "We Found the Guy behind the Viral 'Drunk Pelosi' Video," Daily Beast, June 1, 2019, https://www.thedailybeast.com/we-found-shawn-brooks-the-guy-behind-the-viral-drunk-pelosi-video.
27. Zach Schonfeld, "NRA Spokeswoman Dana Loesch Has Been Railing against Neil Young for More Than 20 Years," *Newsweek*, February 22, 2018, https://www.newsweek.com/nra-spokeswoman-dana-loesch-has-been-railing-against-neil-young-more-20-years-816912.
28. Marlow Stern, "Neil Young Fired Back at His Biggest Troll, Dana Loesch: 'I'm Glad I Got Under Her Skin,'" Daily Beast, March 15, 2018, https://www.thedailybeast.com/neil-young-fires-back-at-his-biggest-troll-dana-loesch-im-glad-i-got-under-her-skin.

29. Sarah D., "Alleged Racist Backlash against *Little Mermaid* Is Only the Latest Example of 'Fake Outrage Bait,'" Twitchy.com, July 5, 2019, https://twitchy.com/sarahd-313035/2019/07/05/ alleged-racist-backlash-against-black-little-mermaid-is-only-the-latest-example-of-fake-outrage-bait-screenshots/.

Chapter 8: A Time for Anger

1. Jacqueline Thomsen, "Booker: Those Who Don't Oppose Kavanaugh Are 'Complicit in the Evil,'" *The Hill*, July 24, 2018, https://thehill.com/homenews/ senate/398681-booker-those-who-dont-oppose-kavanaugh-are-complicit-in-the-evil.
2. Paul Crookston, "McAuliffe: Kavanaugh 'Will Threaten the Lives of Millions of Americas for Decades,'" Washington Free Beacon, July 10, 2018, https://freebeacon.com/politics/ mcauliffe-kavanaugh-threaten-lives-millions-americans-decades/.
3. Eliot A. Cohen, "The Republican Party Abandons Conservatism," *The Atlantic*, September 30, 208, https://www.theatlantic.com/ideas/ archive/2018/09/republican-party-conservative/571747/.
4. Charles J. Sykes, "The Anger of Brett Kavanaugh," *Washington Examiner*, October 2, 2018, https://www.washingtonexaminer.com/ weekly-standard/the-anger-of-brett-kavanaugh.
5. Kenneth P. Vogel and Jeremy W. Peters, "Trump Allies Target Journalists over Coverage Deemed Hostile to White House," *New York Times*, August 25, 2019, https://www.nytimes.com/2019/08/25/ us/politics/trump-allies-news-media.html.
6. Shelby Talcott, "'Extremely Alarming': Journalists Are Worried about Trump Allies Digging Up Their Old Tweets," The Daily Caller, August 26, 2019, https://dailycaller.com/2019/08/26/ journalists-nyt-trump-allies-old-tweets/.
7. "Election of 1800," monticello.org, https://www.monticello.org/site/ research-and-collections/election-1800.

Chapter 9: Make Grace Great Again

1. Dave Boyer, "Pastor Says He 'Hurt' Congregation by Praying for Trump during Unscheduled Visit," *Washington Times*, June 3, 2019, https://www.washingtontimes.com/news/2019/jun/3/ david-platt-mclean-bible-church-pastor-apologizes-/.

2. David Platt, "Prayer for the President," McLean Bible Church, June 2, 2019, https://www.mcleanbible.org/prayer-president.

3. New American Standard Bible, 1995, https://biblia.com/bible/nasb95/1%20 Tim%202.1-6.

4. David French, "Wisconsin's Shame: 'I Thought It Was a Home Invasion,'" *National Review*, April 20, 2015, https://www.nationalreview. com/2015/04/ wisonsins-shame-i-thought-it-was-home-invasion-david-french/.

5. Max Henson, "Muhsin Muhammad Reacts to the Viral Video of Nick Saban That Has Resurfaced," Panthers.com, August 27, 2019, https://www. panthers.com/news/ muhsin-muhammad-reacts-to-the-viral-video-of-nick-saban-that-has-resurfaced.

6. Steve Krakauer, "Rick Sanchez Calls Jon Stewart 'A Bigot'; Says CNN Is Run by Jews," Mediaite, October 1, 2010, https://www.mediaite.com/online/ rick-sanchez-calls-jon-stewart-a-bigot-says-cnn-is-run-by-jews/

7. Conan O'Brien (@ConanOBrien), "CNN's Rick Sanchez said the Jews run CNN. Ah, so that's who we blame for Rick Sanchez," Twitter, 2:58 p.m., October 2, 2010, https://twitter.com/ConanOBrien/status/26199422056.

Index